One of my favorite stories is about the old sea captain who went to his cabin every night, locked the door, took a key and unlocked a small chest, peered inside, then closed the chest and locked it again. His executive officer, stealthily peering in a porthole, often observed the captain doing this.

When the captain died, the executive officer, driven by curiosity, rushed to the captain's cabin, found the key, and opened the chest. Inside, on a small slip of paper were these words: "Port is left, starboard is right."

Sometimes we all forget that which is very important to us and we need to be reminded.

Another Fawcett Crest book
by Dr. Nelson Boswell:

SUCCESSFUL LIVING DAY BY DAY

INNER PEACE, INNER POWER

Dr. Nelson Boswell

FAWCETT GOLD MEDAL • NEW YORK

A Fawcett Gold Medal Book
Published by Ballantine Books

Library of Congress Catalog Card Number: 84-90922

ISBN 0-449-12716-8

Manufactured in the United States of America

First Edition: January 1985

For Maureen, with love

CONTENTS

A PERSONAL NOTE FROM THE AUTHOR

For nineteen years, every day, Monday through Friday, I have performed the same task. I get up early, often in the dark, go to a special room in the house, sit down at an aging typewriter, and write a five-hundred-word script, an essay really, on psychology, mental health, and self-help subjects for my syndicated radio program. Nineteen years, five hundred words a day—the equivalent of over thirty-five books. (Many of the ideas in this book came from this research.)

From time to time I'm asked by a friend, a listener, or a student how I come up with an idea that's interesting and helpful day after day. There's no secret; you work at it, the same as any job. (A famous sports columnist said it was easy writing a daily column. He said you just sit at the typewriter until small drops of blood appear on your forehead.) It's not that hard, but it does require research and reading, trips to the library for study, discussions with men and women in the mental health field, letters to publishers asking for permission to quote various authors, and—always—more research and reading. I also used this research in teaching courses in human behavior at two local universities to graduate students, teachers, and businessmen and women working on a master's degree, and in holding seminars for an organization such as Sales and Marketing Executives.

While researching and writing the syndicated radio program and teaching, I drove sixty miles four or five days a week for three years to a state university, working on a doctor's degree (an Ed.D., Doctor of Education, not an M.D.). When I finally received the degree one subject I continued researching and writing on was learning theory, how people learn, how they block learning, how they internalize knowledge, optimum conditions for learning to take place, how we limit our mental and emotional growth, how habits are formed, how they are broken, why some of us test our limits and go beyond that which we know for certain and others refuse to challenge themselves. I read book after book on this fascinating subject, condensed the ideas, and made the subject easy to understand for listeners and students.

From listener requests for reprints of the scripts on this subject, we could tell that people wanted to make at least some small change in their lives. They wanted to learn and grow, become more comfortable with themselves, be happier. And this was the beginning of Creative Meditation with Positive Programming. (Creative Meditation is an activity that is different from passive meditation. Our family paid a hefty fee for a mantra and instruction in a passive form of meditation. It helped us relax, but since you had to empty your mind of thought, it became boring. One by one we dropped it. Friends of ours said they had done the same.)

Effective learning—just becoming happier, less tense, more forgiving of yourself and others, slowing down, arguing less, giving up perfectionism and "silly guilt" are different ways of *learning*—requires a relaxed, threat-free environment, small bits of information that are internalized, repetition, recall cues, and new habit formation. Creative Meditation with Positive Programming combines all of these elements.

One last thing: even though I used ideas from learning theory, yoga, meditation, autosuggestion, and two or three ideas from previous books of mine, *Successful Living Day by Day*, published by Macmillan and by Fawcett; and *TA for Busy People*, published by Harper & Row, this book is simply written, and the ideas are easy to understand and practice. There is nothing technical about this book. It is not a treatment for illness of any kind. For nineteen years I have been a daily researcher in psychology. This book was written separately from my radio scripts but, like them, is written for busy, active people with practical needs.

Speaking of its being easy to understand reminds me of the story about the farmer. As he came down the steps of the courthouse, he saw a friend, who asked him where he'd been. "Listening to two politicians the past two hours," replied the farmer.

"What were they talking about?" asked his friend.

"I don't know," said the farmer. "They didn't say."

This book isn't like that. You'll know exactly what to do to become happier, more successful, more in control of your life, and to experience greater peace of mind by the time you finish this book. In addition, you will have something to carry away with you, so rather than just reading the book, putting it down, and gradually forgetting it, you will have learned several important techniques that will serve you the rest of your life.

ACKNOWLEDGMENTS

With grateful acknowledgment for permission to quote from the following:

The Anatomy of an Illness, by Norman Cousins (pp. 56, 58, 59, 63, 66), W.W. Norton & Company, Inc.

The Art of Understanding Yourself, by Cecil Osborne (p. 217), Zondervan Publishing House, 1967.

"Barriers and Gateways to Communication," by Carl R. Rogers and F. J. Roethlisberger (July–August 1952), *Harvard Business Review*.

Beyond Biofeedback, by Elmer and Alyce Green, Delacorte Press/Seymour Lawrence.

A Book of Hours, by Elizabeth Yates (p. 29,) Copyright © 1976 by Elizabeth Yates, Seabury Press, Inc., New York.

The Cat-nappers, by P. G. Wodehouse (p. 189), Simon and Schuster.

The Great Divorce, by C. S. Lewis (Copyright © 1946 by Macmillan Publishing Co., Inc., renewed 1974 by Alfred Cecil Harwood and Arthur Owen Barfield).

Health and Human Nature, by Paul Snyder, Chilton Book Company.

Hidden in Plain Sight, by Avery Brooke (p. 40), Harwick Lithograph.

Hope for Man, Joshua Liebman (p. 147), Simon and Schuster.

The Living Talmud by Judah Goldin. Reprinted by arrangement with New American Library, New York.

Man's Search for Meaning, by Viktor E. Frankl (pp. 122, 124), Beacon Press.

Mental Health through Will Training, by Abraham A. Low (pp. 143–145), The Christopher Publishing House.

Motivation and Personality, Second Edition, by Abraham Maslow (p. xxi), Harper & Row Publishers, Inc.

Neurosis and Human Growth, by Karen Horney, M.D. (pp. 57, 58), W.W. Norton & Company, Inc.

90 Days to Self-Health, by C. Norman Shealy, M.D. Copyright © 1976, 1977 by C. Norman Shealy, M.D. A Dial Press Book reprinted by permission of Doubleday & Company, Inc.

Toward a Theory of Instruction (p.3–4), by Jerome Bruner, Harvard University Press.

A Way of Being, by Carl Rogers (p. 81), Houghton Mifflin Company.

Where Have I Been?, by Sid Caesar, Copyright © 1982 by Sid Caesar Productions, Inc., and Bill Davidson, Crown Publishers, Inc.

I owe thanks to Dick and Barbara Smith, longtime friends, who have inspired me in many ways during the writing of this book. Special thanks go to J. T. "Buck" Schrotel for his friendship and advice. The same goes for John Paré, a close friend, who is always willing to lend a helping hand, and to Jose Vivero, Betsy Kennedy, Frank Bloom, and "Bo" Cooksey for special inspiration. I'm also grateful to Louise Desjardins, of Toni Mendez, Inc., who acted as my agent.

My main inspiration while writing this book was Maureen, my wife. Her love, calmness, flexibility, and her constantly positive approach to life have sustained me over the years and made everything possible.

Finally, I wish to thank my three children, Nelson, Kelly, and Sean, now young adults, for the help they gave me and the special insights they furnished.

WHAT CREATIVE MEDITATION AND POSITIVE PROGRAMMING CAN DO FOR YOU

- Teach you how to "program yourself" for happiness.
- Help you break unwanted habits.
- Give you a specific method to reduce stress and eliminate worry and "silly" guilt.
- Heighten awareness of your inner communication; get you in touch with the statements, messages, and suggestions you give yourself and the feelings they cause.
- Show you the way to give yourself positive suggestions that benefit you greatly.
- Suffuse you with a sense of well-being; you become relaxed and often achieve peace of mind.
- Have an abreactive effect—help you to relieve pressure and distress after a series of unpleasant events; calm you down after stress and conflict.
- Sharpen your perceptions; questions and answers become more clearly defined.
- Release your creativity; help you solve problems.
- Renew energy—help relieve fatigue and muscle tension.

I

The Animal Who Talks to Himself

> Man holds an inward talk with himself alone which it behooves him to regulate well.
>
> *Pascal*

Man is the only animal who talks to himself. All day long you carry on an inner conversation with yourself about your problems and opportunities, the people and events around you, the things happening in your life. As you will see, your inner communication is an important part of you; in fact, it *is* you, and it does, indeed, "behoove" you to become aware of it and use it to your benefit. Creative Meditation and Positive Programming will show you how.

An impressive body of research has accumulated on this inner communication, with exciting conclusions.

1

It shows that if we can become aware of and control our inner messages, we can actually change the way our mind and body function. The correct inner messages (along with appropriate medical treatment) can cure and control disease, control pain, cure insomnia, trigger our parasympathetic nervous system, eliminate headaches, and give us renewed energy. Naturally, you must seek first the advice of your medical doctor prior to giving yourself messages to cure illness. Your pain, for example, should not be relieved by you prior to consulting with a doctor, as it may serve as a warning. At any rate, since I'm not a medical doctor, we are not concerned in this book with using Creative Meditation to cure or control disease but with using this technique to give you all the benefits listed at the beginning of this book—in short, to help you become happier, more effective, and give you greater peace of mind.

If the statements, messages, and suggestions you give yourself can cause something as dramatic and profound as tissue changes in your body and thereby help control disease, you can be certain they affect your mental outlook on life and feelings just as profoundly.

Further research shows that, in general, your inner conversation—the messages, statements, and suggestions you give yourself—causes your feelings: up or down, calm or angry, anxious or comfortable, hopeful or pessimistic. What you tell yourself comes first, and then the feeling follows. It often starts with your telling yourself something that causes you to feel a certain way. It gets complicated, because how you then feel colors what you next tell yourself. It's very difficult to change how you feel by attacking your feelings directly, but you can make your feelings more positive by changing the messages you give yourself. I'm not talking about vague, positive attitudes or about positive thinking, which is good as far as it goes, but about a specific and concrete method, Creative Meditation and Positive Programming, to help you become aware of what you tell yourself and the feeling it causes, and to help you change your inner dialogue.

In the field of education, we use the term "behavioral change" with a special meaning. It means not only a change in the way a person acts but includes a change in his thought processes, which, of course, must come first. The problem with some self-help books is that you read them, get an uplifting message, perhaps even try to change a little. Then, within a few days, you'll be back in business at the same old stand, doing and thinking just as before. With this book, I hope you'll experience a permanent change toward greater happiness and inner peace by using a simple exercise, easy to understand and practice, taking so little time that you can practice it daily. It's the daily practice that's important, because in learning and behavioral change, repetition is essential.

When people learn, they don't just soak up knowledge; they are making a change in the way they think and behave. There is really no point in taking in a lot of psychological knowledge if you don't change. And there's no point in changing if it doesn't make you happier, healthier, or more effective in satisfying your needs.

Creative Meditation with Positive Programming, which you'll learn in this book, is exciting, easy to understand, enjoyable to practice, and entirely different from passive meditation. The goal in most forms of passive meditation is to empty your mind. During Creative Meditation your mind is alert and focused, and you perform several interesting activities, the benefits of which are lasting.

With Creative Meditation you don't have to change much or try hard. In fact, you must not try hard. This is the opposite of the way Creative Meditation works. It's easy, because you only make small changes and modifications in the messages, suggestions, and statements you give yourself, and like a ship whose destination is changed greatly by a one-degree change in its heading, you will find a positive change in your life.

It really has to be this way. If nineteen years of research for a syndicated radio program on self-help and psychology, holding seminars for adults (such as sales and marketing executives and educators), and teaching undergraduates and mature graduate students have convinced me of any one psychological fact, it is that few, if any, of us want to or can make great changes in our life-style or daily habits. After all, we have been practicing being ourselves for years and have it down pat.

We all know from personal experience that it's hard for human beings to change, and research proves it, too. Whether it's a habit we want to change, an opinion, a way of handling stress, an attitude that hurts us, whatever, we tend to continue doing things the same, day after day. One famous counselor went so far as to say that most people couldn't change the way they thought and behaved; they were ineducable. That sounds a little harsh, but research does tend to bear this out.

Entering freshmen at a well-known university were given a long questionnaire asking their ideas, opinions, and attitudes on a wide range of subjects. Four long years and many tuition dollars later, they were given the same questionnaire. The results showed that after all this "education," they still held the same opinions, ideas, and attitudes. Very little change in their way of thinking had taken place.

Not Truth but Shadows

If we live in shadows, then shadows are our reality.
Plato

Some people are so rigid they cannot change what they have told themselves about reality even when the facts cry out for a different conclusion. Philip Holzman and George Klein conducted an interesting experiment demonstrating how rigid people can be. They showed the subjects two-inch and five-inch squares. Then they gradually showed the subjects larger squares so that the two-inch square became a three-inch square and the five-inch square became a seven-inch square, then ten inches, and then larger. The subjects were not told the squares were increasing in size.

Some subjects simply couldn't change their original statements. Even though the size of the squares increased, they kept close to their original estimate of the size. If they told themselves it was two inches square, then that's what they kept telling themselves even as the square grew much larger. Especially rigid subjects were estimating squares that were actually thirteen inches on each side to be only four inches on a side! Some people simply can't change the original message they give themselves; it remains the same even in the face of overwhelming evidence to the contrary.[1]

In another interesting experiment, people are shown a series of pictures, one at a time. The first picture is clearly a dog; then each successive picture gradually and almost imperceptibly changes so that in the middle

1. Philip S. Holzman and George S. Klein, "Motive and Style in Reality Contact," *Bulletin of the Menninger Clinic* 20 (1956): 181–91.

of the series, the picture the subject is shown is really half dog and half cat. Many people continue calling the picture "dog" even after the halfway mark, where cat characteristics predominate. It seems that many cannot think "half dog, half cat," and some continue to say "dog" even after the picture obviously shows a cat. These unlucky people are imprisoned in their original perception, much as if a part of their thinking apparatus had been destroyed. They can't or won't change their minds.[2]

Think for a moment about seeing a picture that is half dog, half cat and calling it a dog picture. It seems ridiculous, yet in many ways you and I do this often. We see the man or woman of our dreams, tell ourselves that he or she is a saint, and then, because we told ourselves the wrong thing, end up with a ruined relationship; we see what looks like a dead-end job and later find that someone else made it into an opportunity; we see "hostility" when there is mostly misunderstanding; we see a "bad" person when in truth they are "half bad, half good."

Our Words Have Power

Never forget that the words you use to describe what you believe to be reality are extremely powerful. They determine your life. Tell yourself that you're "not attractive," or that you "couldn't learn that," or, "I don't stand a chance," or, "It's too hard," or, "I've tried everything," or any number of self-limiting statements, and you will then adjust all your efforts to make the statements and messages you give yourself come true.

2. Else Frenkel-Brunswik, "Intolerance of Ambiguity as an Emotional and Perceptual Personality Variable," *Journal of Personality* 18 (1949): 108–143.

(An interesting sidelight here is that research shows there is no correlation between high grades in college and later success, but there is a correlation between the size of a person's vocabulary and success. Many people think this is true because a large vocabulary allows a person to present himself better, make a better impression. There's more to it than that. A larger vocabulary allows a person to perceive reality more precisely. He can give himself a more accurate picture of reality because he has the words to describe it; he can then present this clear picture to others. For example, when I look at my automobile engine, my "automobile I.Q." is extremely low; I have few words to describe the parts and functions. In the same way, you and I cannot think precisely about "snow." To us, it's either snowing, or it's not snowing; we can refine it a little with the words "slush" or "large flakes" or "blizzard." The Eskimos, however, have over one hundred words to describe the fine differentiations of snow that they must be aware of for survival.)

On the other hand, words can blind us. The young child sees miracles all around him: that object hurtling through space and landing in trees is a miracle until we tell him the label is "bird," and then the wonder disappears; wood shooting up out of the ground shrinks in significance when we know it's called a tree; the muscle that, attached to no known power source, pumps in and out, in and out, loses its awesomeness when we call it the heart.

We all see the "truth" differently, but it's deeper than that. What we tell ourselves we see does not conform to reality; rather, we make reality fit what we have already told ourselves is "true." It's even deeper than that, because we don't even *see* reality; we *think* reality because we "see" with our brain and not with our eyes. Our eyes are merely like TV cameras picking up impulses. Our brain takes this raw material, labels it, and subjects it to all manner of unique and singular comparisons and interpretations, and this becomes our "truth."

You Can Tune in on Yourself

If we are happy, productive, able to handle stress, do not worry excessively, have a low level of anxiety, are flexible, get joy from life, take good care of our mental and physical health, and generally operate in our own best interests, then there may be no need to change. But few if any of us fall into all these rosy classifications. At least some of our inner messages are incorrect. We may not be neurotic or emotionally maladjusted, but we all have some rough edges.

Creative Meditation and Positive Programming can help with those rough edges. Creative Meditation gives us a method of tuning in on ourselves to make certain our inner messages serve us correctly, are what we want them to be; life-giving, life-expanding, uplifting, energy filled, free of neurotic overtones or self-defeat. Positive Programming, as you will see, gives us a technique to change our inner conversation for the better; it gives us a specific method to use our conscious desires to change subconscious habit patterns that do not serve us well. In almost twenty years of research and writing in the fields of mental health and psychology *it is the only method I have found to train your subconscious and have some control over it.*

Some Obvious and Destructive Inner Messages

Some of the things we tell ourselves are easy for us to tune in on if we start becoming aware of the statements, messages, and suggestions we give ourselves. In future chapters we'll discuss the inner messages that are difficult to get at, the ones we only become aware of when we become fully relaxed. But for now let's see if we can hear any of the simple messages, the ones that are short and definite, out in the open where we can get at them but so habitual we hardly notice them.

Have you ever heard *you* giving *yourself* any of the following messages:

It's not fair.
I'm sick of trying.
I can't take it.
They have no gratitude.
Just my luck.
He makes me sick.
I can't learn that.
They don't give a damn.
I'm a born loser.
I'll never understand her.
It wouldn't work for me.
I'm too old for that
There's no doubt about it.
They don't like me.
I can never do that.

I can't win.
It's impossible.
That's the way I am.
They don't care about my feelings.
Why even try?
Everything I eat turns to fat.
I've tried everything.
What's the use?
If I want it done right, I'll have to do it.
It's no use talking to him.
That's the story of my life.
Nobody ever listens to me.
Everything I do is wrong.

I mentioned at the start that man is the only animal who talks to himself. The above statements are just a few and the most simple of the many we tell ourselves all day long. Often, in our inner dialogue, we exaggerate our fears, condemn ourselves with guilt, tell ourselves we can't do something and are inferior to others. We give ourselves a message that causes us to feel insecure, unloved, unappreciated, or a victim. We give ourselves messages about ourselves and others that are only partially true, if true at all, and then walk around believing these untruths. The statements and suggestions we give ourselves actually hypnotize us and cause us to act and feel a certain way. They set our attitudes, often rob us of happiness and peace of mind, limit what we will attempt, and determine the quality of our life and sometimes even its duration.

II

Your Inner Communication Can Cause You Trouble

The whole task of psychotherapy is the task of dealing with a failure in communication. The emotionally malad-justed person, the "neurotic," is in difficulty, first, because communication within himself has broken down, and, secondly, because as a result of this his communication with others has been damaged.[1]

Carl Rogers

Whether we are neurotic or not, we believe that what we tell ourselves is reality, but often we come up with falsehoods, incomplete information, half-truths, and sometimes even nonsense. Our conclusions are often slightly or grossly slanted. We go around programming ourselves with our inner statements and messages, and we don't even hear ourselves. We don't sense the full meaning of what we say. We are not even aware that it is *we* who are programming our own minds. And then, when we are feeling down, angry, bitter, or hopeless, we are not aware that it had to happen. We brought it about ourselves. We gave ourselves messages and suggestions that made it happen.

What You Tell Yourself Is What You Feel

Like Hamlet, we tell ourselves tales that harrow our souls. To repeat: the important thing to remember is that what we tell ourselves comes *first* and then our feelings follow.

Our inner conversation, consisting of messages, statements, and suggestions, causes our feelings; it's *not* the other way around. There are events, such as sickness and death, that make us feel sad, threatened, and insecure. These are legitimate feelings, feelings with credentials. But so much of our unhappiness is caused by ersatz feelings—hurt, feelings of inferiority, humiliation, self-contempt, and most fear, anger, and guilt. These are racket feelings, because they don't legitimately get us on with the business of living. They have no legitimate function in our life. These feelings are caused by what we tell ourselves.

This truth, that what we tell ourselves is then what we feel and that this is *our life*, should be engraved on our mirror so that we would be reminded of it every day. It's good news, really, because we can change what we tell ourselves. We can start giving ourselves different messages and make entirely different suggestions to ourselves; and it's not difficult to do. We can wrestle directly with a feeling for years and never change it, but once we identify the statement that causes it and change that statement, the feelings will go away.

When We're Unhappy We're Cognitively Wrong

Many psychiatrists, psychologists, and counselors now maintain that when we are unhappy or anxious, we are not so much emotionally sick as cognitively wrong. In short, they say that when we're unhappy, our inner conversation has run amuck. We're telling ourselves the wrong things about ourselves and about reality, using the wrong words and ideas, perhaps scaring ourselves, putting our problems and opportunities out of focus, calling up the wrong feelings. Naturally, they are not saying that unhappiness or grief caused by the loss of a loved one, or the anxiety we might feel facing the loss of a job or a serious operation, can be brushed off. As I said before, these events cause suffering and must be worked through.

And yet even tragedies in our lives can be lived through better if we give ourselves sustaining and meaningful messages. A woman I know of, after losing three sons, told herself, "I will not be vanquished."

The psychiatrist, Viktor Frankl, lived through the unspeakable horrors of the Nazi concentration camps by telling himself that to survive he must change his fundamental attitude toward life. "It did not really matter what we (the prisoners) expected from life, but rather what life expected from us. We needed to stop asking about the meaning of life, and instead to think of ourselves as those who were being questioned by life—daily and hourly...For us, as prisoners, these thoughts were not speculations far removed from reality. *They were the only thoughts that could be of help to us. They kept us from despair*, even when there seemed to be no chance of coming out of it alive."[2] (Italics mine.)

William James said that the *greatest discovery* of his generation was that human beings, by changing the inner attitudes of their minds, can change the outer aspects of their lives. He continued: *"It is too bad that more people will not accept this tremendous discovery and begin living it."* The quickest and most effective way to change an inner attitude or feeling is to change your inner conversation, to change the messages, statements, and suggestions you give yourself, by practicing the principles of Creative Meditation and Positive Programming.

Giving Yourself the Wrong Message

We all know people who tell themselves the wrong things, people who make life so much harder for themselves than it needs to be. They hold an inner conversation with themselves, make inaccurate statements, give themselves limiting and melancholy messages, and change their life for the worse. Like the mother or mother-in-law who is always hurt; she tells herself, "They don't care about me," and then feels neglected and ignored. The truth is that her children usually care for her deeply, but as she becomes, to use Thurber's phrase, "the Master of the fancied slight," her children start avoiding her. Then there's the son or daughter who says, "No one can tell me what to do," and proceeds to ignore all advice, good or bad. Here are a few more examples:

---

2. Viktor Frankl, *Man's Search For Meaning* Boston: Beacon Press, pp. 122, 124.

"I CAN'T"

A woman told me just last week, "I can't possibly make a speech in front of people." This woman is as interesting and charming as the rest of us but limits herself, in this way and others, with her inner conversation.

"I'LL BE MISERABLE"

"I'll be miserable in Chicago." This statement came from the wife of a friend who is being transferred by his company from Tampa, Florida, to Chicago, Illinois. If she keeps telling herself she'll be miserable, she will be; but she needn't be. Of course, she will miss Tampa, her friends, her routine, the sunshine, but there are more accurate and hopeful messages she can give herself. (I know the message this woman has given herself and the feelings that follow from firsthand experience. I left Chicago twice to move to Florida and twice had to move back to Chicago when things didn't work out as planned.) You do not have to be miserable unless you make yourself miserable. You have adjustments to make; it is disagreeable at first, but *only* disagreeable and only for a short time. *And how bad you feel depends on what you tell yourself.*

"I DON'T HAVE THE ENERGY"

"I simply don't have the energy or time to start a business." This statement came from a man who works at a dead-end job and wants to find another way to make a living. Yet a couple, who are raising three teenage children, found the time and energy. The man works full time for a hospital supply company, but he and his wife have opened a printing shop in a new shopping center. They work hard. One surprise benefit: the business provides a job for each of the three teenagers and gives them spending money. It's too soon to tell how they'll do, but they found the time and energy to try it.

"THEY DON'T WANT ME"

"They only want the young ones for secretaries, not an old bat like me." This statement came from a woman in her middle fifties, recently divorced. Well, sure, many young women are hired as secretaries, but like most negative statements, this one presents only a partial truth. It leaves out the legions of bosses who want experience and maturity, others who don't want to train a young woman and then have her leave to start a family, and still others who respect the judgment of an older woman. (My mother, widowed in her late forties, studied typing and shorthand at a business school in South Bend, Indiana, and after several months of interviewing, landed a challenging job with a real estate developer in the same city. She worked for him, and later his widow, until she was in her middle seventies.)

"THIS IS KILLING ME"

"I can't stand it anymore. I've got to get out." The man who made that statement and I were having lunch at Pier 66, in Ft. Lauderdale, Florida. I had been talking about messages we give ourselves that mesmerize us.

"That's the statement that changed my life for the worse," he said. "We lived in Cleveland. I ran an advertising agency I had started twenty years before. Built it up over the years. But it was hard work, long hours...Some nights, most nights, I'd get home at seven, maybe eight at night, too tired to get out of the car. So I started telling myself, 'This is killing me. I've got to get out.' Well, I finally convinced myself and my wife. I sold the business and moved to Florida, and I've never been as miserable and bored in my life. What I needed was a two-month vacation, or an assistant, or to cut down on my hours, but I thought I was indispensable—what a joke. I was dispensable enough to leave it for good but not for a two-month vacation."

Unhappiness = Habitual Gross Distortion

I could go on with more examples, but I'm sure you have the idea. Start listening to your own statements, both those you make out loud and to yourself, your inner communication. One thing you'll want to bear in mind and always remember: research shows that the thoughts of unhappy, anxious, and depressed people contain *gross* distortions. Unhappy people tell themselves lies and untruths about their lives, their opportunities and setbacks, their friends and family, their luck and mistakes, their odds, their handicaps, the talent, happiness, and resources of others, and then formulate a barely conscious philosophy that, since it does not conform to reality, causes them trouble—and more unhappiness. It's as if they were looking at the world through a dark prism that distorts their view of reality; a prism that filters out a balanced, wholesome view of the *whole* truth. No life-giving, positive rays penetrate the prism.

This negative slant to what we tell ourselves becomes, in time, habitual and in a mysterious way becomes what we want to hear, because it reinforces the conviction that what we tell ourselves is true. The media people know about this morbid fascination, even craving, for bad news, to the extent that print and broadcast media are filled with it. One editor of a large-circulation Florida paper told me that at his newspaper, "Good news is no news."

Our Inner Conversation Must Be Balanced

The answer to the editor is not to print only uplifting, positive news. But he and the media in general would be doing more of a service to the country if the news were not distorted, if it were more in depth and more balanced. It's the same with us individually. Our aim must be to make our inner conversation more balanced, more representative of the truth around us. The answer to the woman who said, "I'll be miserable in Chicago," is not to advise her to say she'll be delighted with Chicago but to bring her around to a more truthful statement about her move. The answer to the advertising man who said, "I can't stand it anymore. I've got to get out," is not to get him to say he doesn't have any problem but to get him to change what he is telling himself so that he can start looking for meaningful solutions and options. Had he been able to break into his inner conversation, which had become a reverberating circuit, he would have operated more in his own best interests and not retired twenty years too early.

Bringing Your Inner Communication Out in the Open

The toast of the nation in the early fifties—that was Sid Caesar. This great comedian brought laughter into the homes of America week after week. And his show was live; there were no second takes, no editing, no "Let's try that again." It was do-or-die, and do they did. But the cost was great. Sid Caesar, partly because of the pressure week after week, started drinking and leaning on drugs.

After eight brilliant and creative years doing *live* television shows, a feat never to be repeated, the end came in 1958; the great Sid Caesar was canceled by his network, and the start of a twenty-year nightmare began.

Twenty years, just a phrase, but a terribly long time when your life is a nightmare. Then, finally, while appearing in a play in Canada, Mr. Caesar became so sick from drinking he couldn't go out for the next act. He knew then that he was killing himself and that he must either decide to live or die.

He told himself he wanted to live and applied his creative genius to solving his problem. In his candid and insightful book *Where Have I Been*, which I highly recommend, Mr. Caesar states that he knew he had to become a friend to himself. He knew that what he needed was to be alone and to talk out loud to himself about his thoughts, feelings, and problems. So he started talking to himself and brought his vague and ill-formed inner messages and conversation out into the open, where he could hear them. He talked out loud to himself in no-nonsense terms, straight, down-to-earth— and even recorded it!

It worked. But let Mr. Caesar tell his story.

On the morning of September 22, 1979, one week after I had arrived, I pulled out my cassette recorder and began a long series of daily conversations with myself. I was very self-conscious at first. For example I had to have the radio on, playing music, before I could start talking. But even on that first day of taping I realized I was

doing a very interesting thing. I had split myself
into two personalities, and I was Sid talking to
Sidney.

Listen as Mr. Caesar talks to himself during one of
his many sessions.

Well, so you want to take a drink? Let's talk
about it. How about a nice good drink? You'll
forget everything, heh? Then you'll think you're
not responsible because then you're a little baby
and they'll have to take care of you, right? You're
a little baby and not responsible, and you can get
angry and do terrible things. Did it ever occur to
you that you use up the same energy being angry
as you do being happy? So do you think it's worth
going through all this, with that boozing you have
in mind? You say yeah, Sidney? Well, you're
wrong, Sidney, outright wrong. You idiot! You
stupid schmuck! Why the hell are you even thinking like this?

Another conversation went like this:

Sidney, you should realize something about your
anger. When you drove your car, you almost
wanted to be in an accident. It was part of the
suicide game you were playing. You wanted to
see how fast, how close you could come...you
had to get even...

Mr. Caesar continued talking to himself, asking specific questions, putting problems in balance, stating
hurts and grievances, countering, shrinking his claims
on life, in general nurturing himself, becoming a friend
to himself.

And then one day, as he and his wife, Florence,
were talking, Mr. Caesar said, "Just like with every-

thing else in my life today, I've changed because, for the first time, I *wanted* to change. Once you make friends with yourself and you feel worthy enough to enjoy yourself enjoying yourself, you try to take advantage of all the 'nows' that come your way."

"Philosophy aside," Florence said, "do you realize it's nearly four years now since you've had your problems with booze and pills?"

"Who's counting," Mr. Caesar replied.[3]

Not all of us are as uninhibited and imaginative as Mr. Caesar; after all, that's his profession—to act things out. And to find out what he was telling himself and then change it certainly worked in his case. But the main point in telling you how Mr. Caesar cured himself of years of drug and alcohol dependence was to show you the profound power of the messages you give yourself. And to show you that you can hear these inner messages, no matter the strength of the spell they cast over you—and hearing them, change them! You don't have to do it out loud, either, as you will see as we get into Creative Meditation. But you do have to keep asking, over and over: "What am I telling myself. Is it the whole truth?"

3. Reprinted from *Where Have I Been?* by Sid Caesar. Copyright © 1982 by Sid Caesar Productions Inc. and Bill Davidson. Used by permission of Crown Publishers, Inc. (pp. 227, 229, 231, 266).

III

The Awesome Power of the Messages You Give Yourself

'Tis the mind that makes the body rich.
Shakespeare

Your Three-Pound Miracle

The placebo, as used in medicine, further proves the tremendous power of the suggestions and statements we make to ourselves. The placebo, usually a combination of milk and sugar, is a harmless pill containing no medicine whatsoever. Over the years, medical science has spent millions of dollars and thousands of hours studying the effects of placebos on patients. The results are truly amazing.

The patient, of course, is never told he is getting a placebo; he is told he's getting medicine that will help him. The patient internalizes this message and tells *himself* that the "medicine" will help him. And lo and behold, he very often gets better. Nobody knows how it occurs, but evidently neurons in the brain, activated by the suggestion, start firing, pathways are formed, networks linked up, perhaps neurotransmitters are released, and Lord knows what else happens.

All of this is easy to believe when you consider the human brain itself. It's a three-pound miracle containing perhaps as many as a trillion neurons, each neuron with as many as ten thousand pathways (unbelievably small tentacles) connecting it to other neurons. The brain is by far the most exquisite and elaborately engineered entity in the entire universe, in charge of the mechanism that carries it from place to place, thinking, observing, storing, deciding, stoking one fire, banking the next, pulsing with self-created energy. And nobody knows how it got wired together. Information in DNA molecules contain the blueprint for the body, but there is no way enough information could be encoded in DNA molecules to tell one neuron in a trillion how to reach another specified neuron in a trillion. Many scientists now think that the wiring instructions come from an outside source.

Tell Yourself There's Hope and a Chemical Change Occurs in Your Body

It doesn't stretch the imagination at all to think of a small number of these neurons, say a mere one million, becoming activated, forming new pathways and networks, and firing off substances because of a suggestion you make to yourself. That's what a placebo is, a suggestion. You're sick; you tell yourself you have taken something that will help you get better, and evidently all sorts of things start to happen in your brain. Think of the placebo as a suggestion that starts the brain working toward a cure. Norman Cousins, in his very helpful book *The Anatomy of an Illness*, makes the following points about the placebo effect:

- The fact that a placebo will have no physical effect if the patient knows it is a placebo only confirms something about the capacity of the human body *to transform hope into tangible and essential biochemical change*. (Italics mine.)
  [Note to reader: Don't pass over the part too quickly about transforming *hope* into tangible and essential biochemical change. *Think of that! You tell your mind there's hope, and a chemical change takes place in your body*.]

- When a patient suffering from Parkinson's disease was given a placebo but was told he was receiving a drug, his tremors decreased markedly.

- During a large study of mild mental depressions, patients who had been treated with sophisticated stimulants were taken off the drugs and put on placebos. The patients showed exactly the same improvement as they had gained from the drugs.

- In a study of postoperative wound pain by Beecher and Lasagna, a group of patients who had just undergone surgery were alternately given morphine and placebos. Those who took morphine immediately after surgery registered a 52 percent relief factor; those who took the placebo first, 40 percent. The placebo was 77 percent as effective as morphine. Beecher and Lasagna also discovered that the more severe the pain, the more effective the placebo.

- Eighty-eight arthritic patients were given placebos instead of aspirin or cortisone. The number of patients who benefited from the placebos was approximately the same as the number benefiting from the conventional antiarthritic drugs.

One interesting study for the die-hard skeptics among us. We might think we're too smart to believe in the power of hope and suggestion. Mr. Cousins said the assumption that there is a correlation between high suggestibility and low intelligence "was exploded by Dr. H. Gold at the Cornell Conference on Therapy in 1946. The higher the intelligence, said Dr. Gold, on the basis of his extended studies, the greater the potential benefit from the use of placebos."

Mr. Cousins says that "In the end, the greatest value of the placebo is what it can tell us about life...What we see ultimately," he says, "*is that the placebo isn't necessary and that the mind can carry out its difficult and wondrous mission unprompted by little pills.*"[1] (Italics mine.)

Your Inner Communication Can Even Cure Disease

Another example of the power your mind has to effect change is the conscious, deliberate "mental manipulation" called Autogenic Training, developed around the turn of the century by Dr. J. H. Schultz, a German psychiatrist.

Dr. Schultz held that by using verbal formulas, you could bring about in yourself, through auto- or self-direction, physiological improvements. Two scientists writing about his work, Dr. Elmer Green and his wife, Alyce, state:

Clinical results have demonstrated that Autogenic Training has helped in the treatment of dis-

1. Norman Cousins, *The Anatomy of an Illness* (New York: W. W. Norton & Co., Inc., 1979), pp. 56, 58, 59, 63, 66.

orders of the respiratory tract, disorders of the cardiovascular system and vasomotor disturbance, disorders of the gastrointestinal tract, and disorders of the endocrine system. It has been effective in the treatment of 60 to 90 percent of patients with long-standing disturbances such as insomnia, headache, bronchial asthma, and chronic constipation, and has proved helpful in behavioral and motor disturbances such as stuttering, writer's cramp, bed wetting, anxiety and phobias.[2]

Dr. Norman Shealy, an internationally famed neurosurgeon, cites research conducted by Dr. Carl Simonton in a test of over three hundred cancer patients who were taught techniques for mentally manipulating their immune mechanism. "The results were that 98 percent of those who practiced the techniques only 15 minutes three times a day experience a shrinkage of their cancers..."[3]

Dr. Shealy says that the nervous system is not a fixed, static thing.

Nerve pathways can be changed. Functions of cells can change or be changed, and if the alteration goes on long enough, a totally new pattern is set up. In the instance of a tumor the *brain can learn to order* the arteries that nourish the tissue to contract and in doing so deprive the tumor of its nourishment and allow it to be reabsorbed and disappear. What you want to do is program your nervous system to set up good patterns, pleasant patterns.[4] [Italics mine.]

2. Elmer and Alyce Green, *Beyond Biofeedback* (New York: Delacorte Press/ Seymour Lawrence, 1977), p. 27.
3. Excerpt from *90 Days to Self-Health* by Norman Shealy, M.D. Copyright © 1976, 1977 by C. Norman Shealy, M.D. A Dial Press reprinted by permission of Doubleday & Company, Inc.
4. Ibid.

Dr. O. Carl Simonton, a radiologist who specializes in the treatments of tumors, and his wife, Stephanie Matthews Simonton, a psychiatric social worker, studied cancer patients who responded exceptionally well to treatment and found that in each case their mental attitude was such that the patients believed their chances of recovery were excellent. Naturally, the Simontons wanted to find a way to teach this attitude to other patients, a formidable undertaking when you realize the terrible depressing effects of the disease itself.

Dr. Simonton, in 1971, started experimenting with a new technique for treating cancer patients who were sent to him for radiation therapy. He tells about his first patient:

> In addition to the medical treatment, I explained to him what my thinking was. I told him how, through mutual imagery, we're going to attempt to affect his disease. He was a 61-year-old gentleman with very extensive throat cancer. He had lost a great deal of weight, could barely swallow his own saliva, and could eat no food. After explaining his disease and the way radiation worked, I had him relax three times a day, mentally picture his disease, his treatment, and the way his body was interacting with the treatment and the disease, so that he could better understand his disease and cooperate with what was going on. The results were truly amazing.[5]

In his excellent book *Health and Human Nature*, Paul Snyder says this about Simonton's experiment:

> Amazing indeed! After three months of treatment, the patient recovered completely. A year

5. O. Carl Simonton and S. Simonton, "Belief Systems and Management of the Emotional Aspects of Malignancy." (*Journal of Transpersonal Psychology*, vol. 7 1975) pp. 29–47. A more complete presentation of the Simontons' work is contained in their excellent book, *Getting Well Again*.

and a half later, there was no sign at all that he had ever *had* throat cancer. This same patient, a feisty and funny gentleman, applied the technique himself to two other things that had been bothering him: arthritis and impotence. He overcame both in the course of his daily exercises in visual imagery.

Such an incident could easily enough be dismissed if it were an isolated case. There are so many unknown factors in cancer, and in arthritis and impotence, for that matter, that any one of a number of things might have coincided with the long, intense period of relaxation and imagery. But it isn't an isolated case. Since 1971 Simonton has treated many cancer patients in this way, while of course simultaneously continuing more traditional treatments.

Simonton reports a case of a 33-year-old woman who was diagnosed as having cancer of the cervix. She refused the usual surgery, which involved removal of the uterus. She had been practicing meditation for some time, and under Simonton's direction she began meditating almost constantly, over a period of months, inducing a self-hypnotic state in which she visualized "a normal, healthy, beautiful uterus." Less than a year after the intensive self-hypnosis began, she was examined again. No trace of the cancer was found.

An Air Force pilot, near death and under treatment for advanced throat cancer, was taught by Simonton to induce the "alpha" state, a measurable condition of bioelectrical activity in the brain that is associated with overall relaxation. The nature of his disease was fully explained to him. He chose a visual image in which the defending white cells were "cowboys" on horseback, attacking and destroying cancer cells pictured as "bandits." The procedure was followed three times a day for fifteen minutes each time. After ten weeks the tumor (which had been the size of a peach) had receded and could not be detected. A biopsy of the patient's throat showed only normal tissue.[6]

Such is the awesome power of the messages and suggestions you give to yourself. But think about it for a moment. Every second of the day and night your brain is monitoring and firing off instructions that keep your heart pumping, your lungs working, blood circulating, your breath going in and out, your body warm and nourished, and a thousand and one other details. It is in touch with every cell in your body, every organ.

If this brain can send messages to run your body, even when you're asleep, and keep everything going; if, along with the proper medical treatment, it can send messages that even cure disease, imagine what you can do in other aspects of your life if you become aware of what you are telling yourself and learn to control and modify your inner communication. Please note that mental imagery is done *in addition* to traditional medical treatment, not *instead* of it. I repeat, if you have any symptoms of illness, see your doctor.

6. Paul Snyder, *Health and Human Nature*, (Radnor, Penn: Chilton Book Company, 1980), pp. 51–52.

IV

Creative Meditation: What It Is and What It Will Do for You

Thinking is the talking of the soul with itself.

Plato

Silence is the element in which great things fashion themselves.

Thomas Carlyle

It's easy to think about thinking *itself when you realize* that almost all thought consists of lightninglike messages inside our minds. We learn to label, classify, memorize, combine, compare, evaluate, sort, synthesize, and retrieve information with *words*.

We all know the power of words. Companies spend billions each year reaching us with their messages. They know the power of those messages and the added power they have if they are repeated. And if you should doubt this power, look around your home and see how many advertised items you've bought.

We know the power our words have on others. They can cheer or anger, soothe or upset, inspire or discourage. Those of us who work with people in any way know we must be careful of the messages we send.

The impressive power of suggestion was demonstrated in an educational research program in which teachers were told that the group of students they would teach were exceptionally bright, which was not true. But sure enough, the teachers treated the students like the stars they had been told they were; after all, when a "genius" asks a stupid question, the teacher must treat it seriously or risk appearing not very bright himself. Not so incidentally, these mediocre students blossomed as a result of the respect and attention given to their thoughts by the teachers.

We have seen in the last three chapters that the messages we give *ourselves* are even more important. Many psychiatrists, psychologists, and professionals in the field of mental health believe that people are neurotic because their inner communication has gone wrong; they tell themselves the wrong thing about reality and then cause themselves to suffer.

The messages and suggestions you give yourself are more than a powerful force in your life; they shape and control your destiny. Your inner conversation *is* your life, and you, in time, become the sum total of what you have told yourself. Your inner messages are, in short, *you*.

Before we go further, let's review what Creative Meditation and Positive Programming can do for you. Even though these techniques are not meant as a treatment for any kind of illness, mental or physical, but are for healthy, active people, the benefits they give you are many.

Creative Meditation and Positive Programming will:

- Teach you how to "program yourself" for happiness.

- Help you break unwanted habits.

- Give you a specific method to reduce stress and to eliminate worry and "silly" guilt.

- Heighten awareness of your inner communication; get you in touch with the statements, messages, and suggestions you give yourself and the feelings they cause.

- Show you the way to give yourself positive suggestions that benefit you greatly.

- Suffuse you with a sense of well-being; you become relaxed and often achieve peace of mind.

- Have an abreactive effect—help you relieve pressure and distress after a series of unpleasant events—calm you down after stress and conflict.

- Sharpen your perceptions; questions and answers become more clearly defined.

- Release your creativity; help you solve problems.

- Renew energy—help relieve fatigue and muscle tension.

Three to ten minutes a day (see chapter XV on three minutes a day), while not optimum, will still be very beneficial. If three minutes is all you can spare, then do it for that length of time. It's better to have short periods of Creative Meditation than none at all. Here again, don't be a perfectionist about it. Take what time you can and enjoy!

We've all heard a number of times that man does not live up to his potential. During the nineteen years

I've been doing research for my syndicated program, I've read well over a hundred books and articles stating that man is not all he could be. Some of them give valuable ideas on how we can improve; others don't. Of course, we're stubborn creatures and resist change, and that is why I've said you can practice Creative Meditation with Positive Programming for as little as three minutes a day. Nobody is so busy that he or she can't spend three minutes a day to achieve greater peace of mind and happiness. Speaking of resisting change reminds me of the story of the county agent who, seeing a farmer ploughing his field, pulled his car over and asked the farmer if he'd read the bulletins from the state, saying that they would help him farm better. "Heck, mister," said the farmer, "I ain't farming now half as good as I know how." Unfortunately, that isn't the problem with most of us; we are living just about as well as we know how, but there is much we don't know about the proper care and operation of the human mind and nervous system.

We have forgotten how to relax; we don't have a method to refresh our mind; we don't know how to make our nervous system our ally; we have no method to solve problems or make decisions; we have no way to objectify ourselves, that is, step outside ourselves and observe what we're telling ourselves; we often have no way to control our thoughts so that they work in our favor and not against us. In learning theory, just for one example, it's well known that many of us spend much energy upon encountering a problem, not in solving it but in refusing to enter the problem and find its exact configuration. This is the opposite of Einstein's approach to a problem. This great man said that to solve many of his toughest problems, he "groped."

We are seldom taught to do this. We are not taught to be tentative (*tentare* in Latin means to "try on for fit"), to hold conflicting ideas comfortably in our mind, to know there are few either/or solutions. From childhood through university we are programmed to come up with answers, answers, answers, and be fast about it. Just imagine, in real life, going to a lawyer, telling him you want help with your problem but only on the condition he doesn't take longer than fifteen minutes and doesn't consult his law books; imagine doing the same with your doctor.

Many years ago William James said that we shouldn't use only our forebrain to come up with answers. Since then, Nobel Prize winners and also geniuses such as Einstein and Edison have solved the most difficult of problems while in a state of relaxation. When you start your Creative Meditation sessions, you'll be pleasantly surprised how, without intense thinking, problems will sort themselves out. You'll often discover a pathway through your problems and be helped with your decisions.

Making Your Nervous System Your Ally

> The greatest thing, then, in all education is to make our nervous system our ally instead of our enemy.
> *William James*

We might wonder why we get upset and nervous and stay that way sometimes over things that are not really that important. Why do these feelings keep banging away inside us long after the event is over? There's a reason. We know that for aeons the answer to any threat for primitive man was to fight or run away— the well-known fight or flight syndrome. Life was dangerous, but at least it was physiologically simple; to run or fight, the heart speeded up, adrenaline flooded the system, the blood prepared to clot to close any wounds, our sympathetic nervous system put us on full alert. Primitive man either ran or fought and in doing so drained off this stress energy; the threat passed, he heaved a sigh of relief, and his parasympathetic system took over and calmed him down.

But in today's world how do you fight or run from a boss who harasses you, a marriage slowly going on the rocks, a child giving you trouble, a lawsuit, a dead-end career. Your nervous system can keep you at semi- or full alert for months! It doesn't have to be something that big, either. In today's complicated and interdependent world you sometimes feel threatened if a computer fouls up your records.

One of the benefits of Creative Meditation with Positive Programming is that it helps counteract the fight or flight syndrome. Relaxation plus Positive Programming helps drain away the feelings of fear, danger, and uneasiness inside us. It calms us down and allows us, if we choose, to review what happened to cause it all in the first place.

We can do this by first achieving a state of relaxation the way I will describe and then listening to the statements, messages, and suggestions we give ourselves.

In just a moment I'm going to tell you about the "Light Touch" cue, and in the next chapter I'll discuss Positive Programming. These techniques, if you practice them regularly, will make a change for the better in your life. But remember, Creative Meditation, Positive Programming, and other techniques in this book are not meant as a treatment for illness. They are for healthy, active people—to help them become happier and more successful, achieve greater peace of mind, and relieve stress and worry. But if you are suffering mentally or physically or if you are deeply unhappy, then do as I would do and seek the help of a professional. I have spent the better part of a lifetime doing research in self-help books, inspirational books, psychology textbooks, and popular psychology books, but if, for example, I suffered an attack of depression or anxiety or was constantly unhappy, I would seek the help of a professional in the mental health field.

The "Light Touch" Cue

One of my favorite stories is about the old sea captain who went to his cabin every night, locked the door, took a key, and unlocked a small chest, peered inside, then closed the chest and locked it again. His executive officer, stealthily peering in a porthole, often observed the captain doing this.

When the captain died, the executive officer, driven by curiosity, rushed to the captain's cabin, found the key, and opened the chest. Inside, on a small slip of paper, were the words "Port is left, starboard is right."

Sometimes we all forget that which is very important to us and need to be reminded. The "Light Touch" cue, though simple, can serve as your recall cue to a relaxed way of living. The philosophy behind the "Light Touch" cue is complicated and important; the cue itself is simple, easy to understand, and easy to make.

The Sicilians make a circle by placing their thumb and forefinger together to ward off evil. You and I are going to use this same sign, but it will be our recall cue to escape the evils of tension and stress by relaxing our body and mind. In addition, since each time you form this circle I want you to just *barely* touch your thumb and forefinger together, this will also be our recall cue to take a "Light Touch" toward life.

Try it now. Place your thumb and forefinger together so they just barely touch and relax your body and mind as you do it. From now on, do this a number of times each day, and every time you make this sign, smile. It's difficult to smile without relaxing. In the next chapter we'll add to this relaxation technique your Positive Programming message. But for now practice your "Light Touch" several times so that you'll remember this simple but effective recall cue.

How to Relax for Your Creative Meditation Session

To practice Creative Meditation, you must relax. You do not have to close your eyes and drift down into another state of consciousness. You have a choice, and there are reasons for this. The main reason is that I want you to be able to meditate in the same mode you do other things in your life. In addition, a number of people I know either don't like to meditate with their eyes closed or won't take the time. I've also been told by several people who practice passive meditation that they consider meditation separate from the rest of their life. I want Creative Meditation to become part of your life so that even in the middle of a meeting you could, on cue, if you wished, relax, look out the window, and for a few moments practice Creative Meditation. You can choose which way you find more comfortable and effective and which best suits your circumstances.

The following, then, shows you how to become relaxed for a full or instant Creative Meditation session.

FOR A FULL SESSION

1. Select a quiet place where you will be free from distractions. If you're at home, this could be your

bedroom, for example, or if you are at the office, perhaps you can close the door while you meditate. If
you can't get off someplace by yourself, don't worry
about it, and remember, since you may leave your
eyes open if you wish, no one will know what you are
doing.

2. Get as comfortable as you can. Perhaps in your
favorite chair if you're at home.

3. Give yourself the cue to relax, as I just described,
by placing the thumb and forefinger of one hand together in a circle, just barely touching. This is your
signal to yourself to relax and take a "Light Touch"
approach to life.

4. Take several deep, comfortable breaths. Breathing
slowly and deeply a few times has a calming effect.
Do it only once if you prefer. Some people feel a little
dizzy if they take too many deep breaths.

5. Relax all over. Become aware of tightness in your
body and let each muscle relax. If you're sitting in a
chair, picture yourself melting into it. Tell yourself
that tension has no place in your life, that it's not the
way to live or work. Tell yourself how much better
you'll feel and how much more you can get done and
enjoy doing it if you are relaxed. I'm reminded of a
story I heard about a famous ro football player. After
he carried the ball for a sizable gain, he always walked
very slowly back to the huddle. A sportswriter asked
him why he did this, and the player answered, "I get
paid for running; they don't pay me anything for walking back." You might remind yourself that tension
doesn't pay off, either.

Let each muscle relax. Start with your forehead
and work your way down your body: your eyes, facial
muscles, jaws, neck, shoulders, arms, hands, stom-
ach, legs, and feet. It sometimes helps to tighten up
your muscles and then relax them and feel the difference. Let go. Let go. For the duration of your session,
do not exert effort. Feel your limbs getting comfortably heavy, warm, loose, and limp.

6. For a few moments think about how relaxed you are, how comfortable you feel. Tell yourself what a good thing it is to nurture yourself. Imprint on your memory how exhilarating it is to be at peace. Accept yourself *unconditionally*.

FOR AN INSTANT SESSION

1. Here again, you may keep your eyes open. You can have an instant Creative Meditation session almost anyplace it's safe for you to let your mind wander for a few seconds. Your instant session can last as long as you want, but I call it instant because usually it will be of short duration, say, from several seconds to several minutes. These short sessions give you an opportunity to ask what you are telling yourself and then repeat your Positive Programming message, which you will learn about in the next chapter.

2. Give yourself your "Light Touch" cue, forming a circle with thumb and forefinger barely touching. Remember, this is your signal to yourself to have a light touch, to let go and relax.

3. Breathe deeply and comfortably several times to help you relax.

There is a good chance that you just might be a bit of a perfectionist. Many of us who read self-help books are often driven by our inner tyrant to do things perfectly and, on top of that, to do them in less time than it would take an ordinary mortal. Don't be perfectionistic about your Creative Meditation session. There is no perfect way to do it. Experiment with the steps that help you relax, find the method that is best suited to you and that you are comfortable with, and then continue with that. You will have times when you relax quickly and easily. You will have other times when you think that it is not working for you. You will have sessions that seem mediocre; at other times, you will feel very good about your session.

Now that you are relaxed, sitting comfortably in your chair, there are several things you can do in your Creative Meditation session, all of them interesting and beneficial. These are imaginative ways of giving yourself inner space.

You Can Float in Your Creative Meditation Session

We all need silence—both external and interior—to find out what we truly think.

Shirley Hazard
The New York Times Book Review
November 14, 1982

Floating is just what the name implies; you're relaxed, free and easy, going with the stream of your mind, letting what wants to pass through it pass through. You let go and let be.

When a particular feeling washes over you, if it's a positive feeling, you may wish to dwell on it for a moment or two, allow it to make you happy, let it nurture you. If it's a negative feeling, then you must push it from your mind. If you are going to have an effective Creative Meditation session, then you must not dwell on negative feelings. As you dismiss the negative feeling, you may wish to tell yourself that it is "only a feeling" and thereby rob it of its power. Or you might wish to tell yourself that "feelings are not facts" and with that push the feeling away as much as you are able and replace it with a Positive Programming message (see chapter V).

As you float, gently, without effort, tune in on yourself. Listen to the messages and suggestions you give yourself. Ask yourself if your inner communication contains the truth, the whole truth, and nothing but the truth.

You Can Visit a Haven in Your Creative Meditation Session

Another activity you may wish to engage in during your Creative Meditation session is that of visualizing yourself in a pleasant haven. Many people find a special peace this way. While sitting in your comfortable chair with your eyes open or closed, depending on your preference, you picture yourself in a place that you find comforting and secure, free from pressure and distraction.

I'll give you a personal example of how to do this part of your Creative Meditation session. A number of years ago, I lived in an apartment in a place called Tudor City. Tudor City consists of ten or twelve high-rise apartment buildings in the heart of New York City, clustered together in several blocks around 42nd Street and the East River. It's a city in itself, isolated from the hubbub of the larger city it's a part of. The rent was low because of rent control, but the view from my windows befitted a millionaire. One window looked out over the East River, and another window looked out over the United Nations building. And all of this was only a fifteen-minute walk to the Columbia Broadcasting System office where I worked.

Today, years later, this is the place I revisit in my mind. Once I have begun my Creative Meditation session, it only takes me a few seconds to revisit this apartment in my imagination. I can picture Tudor City and the apartment as it was, hear the faint sound of traffic noises coming from below, and recreate the scene so that I am there in every sense except physically.

I picture myself walking down the long hallway to the apartment, opening the door, closing and bolting the lock for privacy, and then, high above the city, picture myself, peaceful and secluded, far away from the stress and strife of the workaday world.

Your haven can be anything you choose just so long as it's serene and peaceful. Some have told me they have a place at a lake, others a secluded spot in the woods, a boat, a room at a lodge. I was surprised when a woman told me her haven was the beach. When I think of the beach, I picture all sorts of distractions, but she considers it quiet and restful.

You Can Commune with Yourself or with a "Wise Friend" in Your Creative Meditation Session

You can visualize, either while floating or in your haven, communing with yourself or with a "wise friend." This must be a slow, gentle question-and-answer activity. The questions must not be aggressive, and answers must not be demanded.

The wise friend, of course, is a part of your personality, but some people find it helps them to ask and answer questions by this device of the imagination. Your wise friend is always calm, nurturing, and accepting. Among other benefits, whether you commune with yourself or a wise friend, it helps you to objectify yourself and your problems. It's a device whereby you can step outside yourself and take a look at yourself.

Also, it's a good method of listening to your inner voice.

Contemplative Listening in Your Creative Meditation Session

And Wisdom's self
Oft seeks to sweet retired solitude,
Where, with her best nurse Contemplation,
She plumes her feathers, and lets grow wings.

John Milton

During your Creative Meditation session you can spend either part of your session or all of it in Contemplative Listening. It's difficult for us in these times to sit with no distractions and quietly let our thoughts drift in and out of our mind. We are so accustomed to the noise, blare, and rush of modern times we forget to be alone with ourselves, quiet and inactive. We even get irritated when someone gets ahead of us in traffic; we buy "instant on" TV sets so that we don't have to wait the few seconds for the set to warm up. Talk about jerk and snap!

One way to learn how to use your mind more fully is to sit still and listen to it. Focus on one thing at a time and listen to what you tell yourself about it. Take "love." For a minute or so focus on love. What do you tell yourself about it? Do you think it important? Do you think all it means is the thrill of lovemaking, or is it deeper than that? Does it contain an element of wishing to care for a person? Is that why much of what masquerades as love is false? How far should your love go? To just family, friends, people like you, or the whole human race? How do you show your love? Are you able to give and accept love? When you love someone, are you acceptant and nonjudgmental? What do they mean when they say that God is love?

Do you see the possibilities for Contemplative Listening? There are hundreds of other questions you can ask yourself about the one subject of love alone. You can do the same with any number of other subjects, such as your goals, bad habits, friendship, hostility, hurt, anger, embarrassment, guilt, marriage, children, fear, grief, or sex; the list is endless. There is a chapter in this book titled, "What Do You Ask Yourself in Your Creative Meditation Session?" You can pick out a subject there that you would like to explore and then, in your session, gently ask what you are telling yourself about this particular subject and keep focused on it for either part of your session or all of it. Always remember to end your session with Positive Programming.

Only You Can Decide

When the pupil is ready the teacher will come . . .
Ancient Chinese saying

A friend told me about her experience during Creative Meditation sessions.

Sometimes it is a religious experience for me. I occasionally have experiences during my sessions that could best be described as spiritual, sort of "another world" experience. I get answers, suggestions, and insights I would not ordinarily have thought of. Often I get a mysterious and strange comfort from talking with my "friend." Sure, I know it's me talking to me, but at times it seems to have an added dimension.

The spiritual or religious part is for you to decide. If it bothers you, leave it alone. I've discussed this with a few people from a wide range of religious thought. A number of them say, in effect: the God they worship would resemble, if he resembled anything a mere human being could imagine, an intelligence. They go on to say that if you believe in a supreme intelligence, it does not stretch credulity that while you are relaxed, open, and receptive, searching quietly for truth, you might receive insights and inspiration. It can be a very effective form of prayer.

You can take it from there, and if it doesn't fit your point of view, leave it alone. Whatever you attribute it to, from time to time you will experience something reassuring, something helpful and comforting.

> ...I have felt
> A presence that disturbs me with the joy
> Of elevated thoughts; a sense sublime
> Of something far more deeply interfused,
> Whose dwelling is the light of setting suns,
> And the round ocean and the living air,
> And the blue sky, and in the mind of man;
> A motion and a spirit, that impels
> All thinking things, all objects of all thought,
> And rolls through all things.
>
> *Wordsworth*

It's Your Session

Remember that your Creative Meditation session is not a precise drill. During any one session you may float awhile, then visit your haven and ask questions of yourself while there, then ask questions of your "wise friend," listen for answers, and so on. If your time is short, relax, give yourself the "Light Touch" cue, and then ask yourself only one or two questions, such as, "Why am I nervous about this upcoming meeting? What am I telling myself about it?" Then give yourself the Positive Programming message that you will do well and stay relaxed; visualize yourself doing well.

For your sessions there is no "right" sequence, no exact way to do it. There are only three things you must do: You must give yourself the "Light Touch" cue and immediately relax all over, you must gently push negative thoughts from your mind while asking what you are telling yourself to cause the negative thought, and you must end your session with a good message from the Positive Programming chapter, or you may wish to make up your own Positive Programming message.

Before we go into the Positive Programming chapter, let's review for just a minute the steps in Creative Meditation:

The "Light Touch" Cue	You do this before you start every session. This is your recall cue to remind you to relax and take a "light touch" toward life. You may also use the "Light Touch" cue during the day without having a session, to remind you to relax and to slow down.
Relax all over.	You do this every session.
Ask what you are telling yourself to cause a certain feeling.	You do this when it's applicable. You always do it when you feel negative or unhappy.

You commune with yourself. You commune with a "wise friend." You float. You practice Contemplative Listening.	These activities intertwine with each other and fade in and out. You'll be communing with yourself, for example, and be practicing Contemplative Listening at the same time.
Positive Programming	You do this every session.

One More Time, Keep It Simple

If you've ever taught (and almost all of us are teachers with our family, our friends, our coworkers, in that we give each other information all the time and strive to be understood), you know that if someone is to learn something you must make it simple and start from where the student is and build from there. So please keep all we've been discussing simple in your mind. Creative Meditation is the name for the whole process. You can do it for short or long periods of time. You give yourself a "cue" to relax, then there are the three or four interesting ways to meditate, which I have described, and you end with Positive Programming. That's all there is to it, and you don't have to do it perfectly. But repetition is important, so please do it every day to develop the habit and make it part of your life.

V

The Power of Positive Programming

The personhood of man, therefore, is an interinvolvement of rich intercommunication or dialogue. Man, though he feels lonely, is always in encounter with himself. The more he presses this dialogue of the self, the deeper he goes into the self itself.

St. Augustine

The highest possible stage in moral culture is when we recognize we ought to control our thoughts.

Darwin

Do you like the idea of positive thinking? Of course you do. It's impossible to argue that positive thinking isn't a good way to live. It's a wonderful idea. The problem with positive thinking is that it often doesn't make a behavioral change in a person. When you get hurt, angry, embarrassed, pessimistic, guilt-ridden, disappointed, worried, fearful, hopeless, involved in the self-torture game, by definition you can't think positively, because you're swamped in negative feelings.

With Positive Programming you train your subconscious. You select a goal you consciously desire to reach and by verbally repeating the goal to yourself many times you imprint it in your subconscious. (Once you have done this you will have changed the pattern of your inner communication.)

Positive Programming is based on the learning principle that if you keep a message unit short and simple and repeat it many times it becomes a part of you, deeply imprinted on your mind. Repeat a simple phrase like "I accept myself unconditionally," say it over and over, many times a day, day in and day out, think about it when you say it, and you will see a change take place in yourself.

Do it now. Completely relax yourself. Feel your facial eye, neck, shoulder and arm muscles go lax, put everything out of your mind, and then repeat to yourself five to ten times, "I do the very best I can...I accept myself unconditionally...I like myself." Just doing that, you'll feel better, you'll also feel something taking place very quietly inside you, an interior reverberation, a good feeling.

You are giving yourself a good message. Instead of the usual rushed, strained and negative litany of all your shortcomings you are doing something for yourself that all of us must do for mental health; you are accepting yourself. You already know that others can say things that have the power to either hurt you or make you happy. You have the power to do it to yourself.

William James said, "I have no doubt that most people live, whether physically, intellectually or morally, in a very restricted circle of their potential being. They *make use* of a very small portion of their possible consciousness, and of their soul's resources in general, much like a man who, out of his whole bodily organism, should get into a habit of using and moving only his little finger."

We have within us a cybernetic system (*cybernetic* is Greek for steersman) that operates like an airplane on automatic pilot. Give that internal cybernetic system of yours the goal, repeat it so it sinks in, and without knowing it you will make subtle adjustments and unconscious decisions to decisions to steer toward your goal. The goal can be something as subtle as becoming comfortable with yourself, getting along with your friends or your children, developing a more positive attitude toward life. These goals must be encoded in a short statement, and repeated many times so they become an automatic response, and that's where Positive Programming comes in.

In short, you program yourself, and if you don't like the word "program", remember that it is *you* who sets the goals, you are the one who does the programming. Set the goal to be that of accepting yourself unconditionally, for example, encode it into the short statement I mentioned earlier, repeat it over and over day after day and things begin to happen on a subconscious level; you relax more, become less critical of yourself and others, let up on your perfectionism, perhaps stop feeling the constant pressure of time passing because you're not so hard on yourself, you start enjoying yourself, others, and your life more. They in turn feel more comfortable with you, they sense a change, let their guard down, become more intimate and friendly. You respond with increased warmth and feel even better about yourself, a thousand and one subtle adjustments take place both on the conscious and unconscious level and so your simple little message, "I accept myself unconditionally" brings all sorts of changes in your life and rolls on with no end in sight. Other Positive Programming messages bring about desirable changes of a different nature.

Positive Programming gives you an automatic reflex; you *program* the reaction you want by repeating it many times until it becomes part of your conscious and unconscious mind. (The Positive Programming phrases come later in this chapter.) You don't need to be a learning expert to see that a short phrase that has meaning to you, repeated many times, will become a habit. In time it will become a message you give yourself automatically, without even thinking: you will have made a behavioral change in yourself. (Remember your teacher drilling the multiplication table into your head through repetition? She didn't go over it with you just once. It was the same when you learned to read, which reminds me of a humorous story about a man who said he learned numbers in school but not the alphabet, so that when he saw a road sign, he always knew how far it was but never where to.)

With Positive Programming you select a message from this chapter (or you can make one up if you wish) and repeat it many times during the day and in your Creative Meditation sessions. After many repetitions the message becomes a part of you, encoded in your mind. It becomes something *you tell yourself*, and in time it will be a lightninglike response when you need it. You will automatically think of your message and the philosophy it represents. The message will be you, and you will be the message, and it will penetrate the deepest level of your mind. You will have trained your subconscious. You will retrieve this message and play it for yourself automatically when you need it, the same as you can retrieve that part of the multiplication table you need.

Let's see how this works with another example. Take the simple Positive Programming message, "I Choose Happiness." (This message is not as simple as it seems, as you'll see in a minute.) In learning-theory terms, "I Choose Happiness" is merely a recall cue to the more complicated philosophy behind the message. Constant repetition of the message until it becomes a part of you ensures that you'll remember your approach to life, or what Gordon Allport terms your "style" or "selective set."

A Bad Habit Blocks All Other Responses

Positive Programming works because if we take a short phrase, one that expresses our philosophy, and repeat the phrase over and over for a long period of time, that phrase and the philosophy it represents will become part of us and will extinguish negative habits of thought that hinder us. And when you think about it, why shouldn't we program ourselves? Others are constantly trying to program us: teachers, friends, television, radio, magazines, newspapers, books, parents, and politicians. There is even a school of psychological thought that holds that we become what others tell us we are, that we receive a stream of "reflected appraisals"* from childhood on, and these reflected appraisals form our self-concept, good or bad, comfortable or tortured. Dwell on that for just a moment: You are the sum total of what others have said you are. What a preposterous way to live! Luckily, there's a way out. Once you become aware of this *pre*programming, you can *re*-program.

It's interesting to note that research in learning theory proves that a habit effectively blocks all other responses. You can't, in other words, extinguish, say, a pessimistic approach to life merely by resolving to be

---

*The theory of psychiatrist, Harry Stack Sullivan.

hopeful and optimistic, because your pessimism blocks other responses. It's like the political truism that in an election you can't beat a somebody with a nobody but only with another somebody. But with repetition and focus you can gradually imprint another habit, one that becomes stronger. In the split second before your feelings take over, you can respond with "I Choose Happiness" and thereby give yourself a different inner message in place of your usual pessimistic response. One major difficulty in breaking the pessimistic habit is becoming aware of it and at the same time realizing its pathological nature. We are inclined to think that pessimism is the prudent way to live, or we have had more than our share of bad luck to justify that position. Yet there are any number of realistically cautious people and also people who have suffered terrible blows from fate who still remain hopeful and happy.

The Good Positive Programming Messages

The following are Positive Programming messages you should repeat to yourself in your Creative Meditation session, when your mind is relaxed, alert, and suggestible, and also when you are walking around going about your business. Remember, only one message per session, and stick with that one message for as long as it takes to become your automatic response.

So, select one or two of these messages, depending on your life situation at the moment, and make it a part of you. An especially effective time to repeat your message is at the end of either your full or instant Creative Meditation session. If you think it might be helpful, tell a member of your family or a close friend what your message is (not everyone will want to do this) so they can remind you of it when you are under unusual stress. Another effective time is right before you go to sleep. Make it part of your nighttime prayers.

The messages are in capital letters so that in the future you can find them for easy reference. While you are in your Creative Meditation session, you may very well be given a hopeful message or suggestion different from the following, a message that is tailor-made to fit your specific problem of the moment, one that is distinctly for you. That message or suggestion, if it is positive and life-enhancing, may be the one you wish to repeat and imprint on your mind.

"DON'T MAKE IT IMPORTANT"

"... Jeeves," I said, "... Do you ever brood on
   life?"
"Occasionally, sir, when at leisure."
"What do you make of it? Pretty odd in spots,
   don't you think?"
"It might be so described, sir."

P. G. Wodehouse[1]

It's difficult to keep a sense of proportion in our lives, to remember that it is indeed "odd in spots," but the Positive Programming message, "Don't make it important," can help. We strive to get ahead, to do right, to make ends meet, to get along, and before we are aware of it, our life is an endless struggle. Everything seems important and upsetting: a boss's frown, a neighbor's unfriendliness, a child's rudeness, a friend's forgetfulness, a dental appointment, an unfair advantage taken by an associate, and to top it off, we think we may not be quite as healthy as we were; we

1. P. G. Wodehouse, *The Cat-nappers* (New York: Simon and Schuster, 1974), p. 189.

know we're getting older, and we suspect we're getting nowhere. "Don't make it important" can be used for the thousand and one events in our lives that irritate, worry, or upset us, and it can force us to shrink our problems to proper size.

A corollary to "Don't make it important" is "See the humor." To paraphrase Mark Twain, man is the only animal who can laugh...and the only one who needs to. There is often a split second when, instead of getting angry, nervous, or unhappy, we can choose to see the humor in a situation.

Abraham Lincoln was an outstanding example of a person using humor to keep himself calm. All during the terrible events of the Civil War he told humorous stories. (One of my favorites is Lincoln's story about the man who advertised that he had made a discovery by which he could make a new man out of an old one and have enough of the stuff left over to make a little yellow dog.) When he was criticized for telling jokes during a crucial stage of the war, he replied, "Sir, I laugh so I won't cry."

You and I need to do that. We need to laugh so we won't get angry or critical or worried or upset.

The "Don't make it important" message tells you to minimize the importance in your life of those negative situations and irritating people you come up against and not blow their significance out of proportion. It gives you an automatic cue to reduce your problem to a minimum.

"I CHOOSE HAPPINESS"

I hesitated to suggest this Positive Programming message. On the surface it sounds too much like a silly bromide—skip merrily along, and all you need do is decide to be happy, and lo and behold, happiness is yours.

I'm not using "I choose happiness" in that sense, but in the sense that you tell yourself you choose happiness *instead* of other ways of thinking; the emphasis is on choice. You are reminding yourself, each time something comes up that could cause you to lose your peace of mind, that you do have a *choice*. For example:

I choose happiness instead of getting angry (at your friend, spouse, child, co-worker, etc.).

I choose happiness instead of putting myself down.

I choose happiness instead of worrying about my work.

I choose happiness instead of fear (about my health or growing older or dying).

I choose happiness instead of————. (You fill in the blank.)

Remember to tell yourself to "choose happiness" about small details in your life rather than arguing with the garage attendant or worrying about your next dental appointment. There is no point in ruining an entire morning because you had a useless argument with someone, or spoiling a whole week worrying about an upcoming dental appointment that lasts an hour.

Also, remember that you will not necessarily choose happiness and then automatically feel happy. Happiness, for all of us, is episodic; it comes and goes, and very often its visit coincides with your being actively engaged in something that interests you. The frequency, depth, and duration of those episodes can be increased, however, if you give yourself the right messages, suggestions, and statements.

A woman who could not see, hear, or speak made the decision to choose happiness. Helen Keller made the statement, "I have found life so beautiful." She chose to be happy. We all know people with handicaps and burdens who seem to be happy in spite of their troubles. Yet when you analyze them, very often they are happy not in spite of but because of their handicaps. Their handicap forces them to find that which is beautiful, to find the essence in life and ignore peripheral irritations. Helen Keller made a life for herself in her mind.

From time to time we should ask ourselves, "How am I being a problem to myself?" "What do I do to cause my unhappiness?" "How do I destroy my own peace of mind?" We each have our unique ways of sabotaging ourselves. As Hannah Smith said:

> The greatest burden we have to carry in life is self; the most difficult thing we have to manage is self. Our own daily living, our frames and feelings, our especial weaknesses and temptations, our peculiar temperaments, our inward affairs of every kind—these are the things that perplex and worry us more than anything else, and that bring us most frequently into bondage and darkness. In laying off your burdens, therefore, the first one you must get rid of is yourself. You must hand yourself, with your temptations, your temperament, your frames and feelings, and all your inward and outward experiences, over into the care and keeping of your God, and leave it all there. He made you, and therefore He understands you, and knows how to manage you; and you must trust Him to do it.[2]

In your Creative Meditation sessions you might ask how you yourself spoil your hours and days. Is pride your downfall? Are you overly concerned with what

2. Hannah Whitall Smith, *The Christian's Secret of a Happy Life* (Old Tappan, New Jersey: Fleming H. Revell Company, 1952), pp. 38, 39.

others think? Is striving for power, prestige, or position your weakness? Will you incur any amount of tissue damage to yourself, any amount of strain and tension for money? Perhaps inferiority feelings rob you of happiness. Do you crave affection or approval to the extent you feel rejected if you don't receive it? Do you drive yourself to higher and higher levels because you're obsessed with the fear of failure? Are you so fearful of being hurt you turn away from all relationships? Are you so driven by the need to be perfect that you live in fear of making a mistake? Are you living behind a self-created facade that causes you uneasiness? Are you trying to live up to the expectations of others?

Choosing happiness does not require that you immediately gratify every wish. We all at times decide to pay a price, to delay gratification, in order to reach a goal. I remember calling an author of self-help books who has since died and asking him to dinner. (The main thrust of his books was that if you want something, you ought to have it; you should indulge yourself immediately and never mind obligations and discipline.) He replied to my invitation, "Nelson, I'd love to get out of this prison I've put myself in. But I've promised myself I won't leave this room until I get this book finished. It'll take about another three months." I thought, as I hung up, if the readers of his books knew the discipline and capacity for self-denial this man has, they would laugh at his philosophy to "do your own thing the minute you want to do it and whenever you want to do it."

And yet this man is not false or insincere. We must all postpone happiness from time to time, or we wouldn't even mow our lawn, let alone write a book. But the question you must ask yourself is: Have you chosen a way of life where you are *constantly* postponing happiness and peace of mind? Is this your *dominant* decision? Are you always putting off living until some distant day in the future when there is a good chance it will be too late?

By repeating the phrase "I choose happiness," you tell yourself that you have decided not to put off *living*, that you will no longer be a problem to yourself and stand between yourself and a calm, fully functioning life. You tell yourself that you are going to live *now*, enjoy *now*, and no longer postpone your life to chase after wind.

"IT IS NOT 'UNFAIR', IT JUST 'IS'"

Later in this book I quote the renowned psychiatrist, Dr. Karen Horney, as saying, "Any hardship becomes ten times harder if we consider it unfair." If you think in terms of "fair" or "unfair" it adds to your problem the terrible feeling that you have been put upon by fate or family or friends. You then must live through whatever disagreeableness is involved, and, if you tell yourself it's unfair, you must also bear the feeling that you are a victim. You have turned your problem into two problems, and because unproductive feelings are involved, you have magnified both.

During the annoying and troublesome events of your days, shrug them off by repeating to yourself the message "It is not 'unfair'; it just '*is*.'"

"IT'S ONLY DISAGREEABLE AND I CAN HANDLE THAT"

I've said before that many of us allow our fearful imaginations to conjure up all sorts of images that spell danger and disaster. We tell ourselves that something that, in truth, will only discomfort us or annoy us or be disagreeable or a small pain, is something to be fearful of, think about obsessively, and worry ourselves to death about.

Of course there are disasters that occur in our lives,

but when they do, for the most part, they usually hit us from the blind side and are not the things we were fussing and stewing about, anyway. Many of us make very heavy weather out of minor problems. It's not only foolish to whip yourself up when you don't need to, but it is a dangerous mental activity, and it becomes a habit. In his excellent book, *Mental Health Through Will Training*, Abraham A. Low says:

> If the nervous patient is to rid himself of his disturbing symptoms he will have to cultivate the Will to bear discomfort. Time was when bearing discomfort was considered part of life, a part accepted by everybody and practiced everywhere...
> This calls for an attitude which, far from exalting the virtues of comfort, places the emphasis where it belongs: on the WILL TO BEAR DISCOMFORT.[3] [Capital letters are Dr. Low's.]

In your Creative Meditation sessions give yourself the message that you can bear discomfort. Tell yourself that something will only be disagreeable and you can handle that.

A close friend of mine was at one time the head writer for a famous comedian. When I knew Al, he was always calm, judicious, and understanding; a remarkable person. One day, when I mentioned his calm

---

3. Abraham A. Low, *Mental Health Through Will Training* (Boston: The Christopher Publishing House, 1950), pp. 143–145. I recommend this book for those suffering from mental or emotional problems, in addition to seeking professional help. Dr. Low is the founder of Recovery, Inc., which operates in many cities around the world. You might wish to check it out and, after doing so, attend one of their meetings to see if it could help you or a loved one. I checked with their local chapter and was told there is no charge for attending the meetings other than a free-will offering at the end; you can contribute as much or as little as you please. If you are under the care of a professional, ask him or her first whether they think this might help you or not.

approach to life, he said, "It's taken me thirty years to learn to shrug my shoulders." Al was perhaps the most intelligent person I have known, yet much of his philosophy was contained in that simple shrug, and it helped him cope with a financial reversal, a family problem, betrayal by two of his friends, and the problems of belonging to a minority. He not only coped but rose above his problems.

"STRAW INTO GOLD"

If you are having trouble getting along with someone, tell yourself that you will turn their straw into gold. Every time you deal with them remind yourself of your "straw into gold" message. It works best with a friend or a loved one, but at times it can be used with people you merely work with.

How do you go about turning straw into gold? A big part of it is your attitude. If you take the attitude that you can agree with at least a small part of what the other person is saying, you can build from there. You take that ten percent, say, that you can agree with and nurse it as you would a small flame; you cherish what the other person says. And, of course, another part is that you become accepting and open. You accept what the other says as much as you can, and you throw the best possible light on it.

A mother told me about berating her seventeen-year-old son because he never seemed interested in what she and the boy's father were doing, never said anything about his activities, and did no work around the house. He would help when asked but never thought of doing any chore on his own. One evening, she said, she and her son were in a relaxed mood, and rather than speak to him as parent to child (this is how we so often speak to our children even when they are grown and then wonder why they don't share their lives with us), she decided to withhold all criticism and judgmental attitude and talk to him as one adult to another. Their conversation became very intimate and meaningful, just two people trying to get from here to there in life, telling about their hopes and fears.

"I told him, in quiet, non-guilt-producing terms, about some of my real problems," she said. "Things that bothered me. Not accusations against him but rather personal concerns about my health, my husband's health, and his job. I told him I was thinking of going back to work to take the financial strain off his father.

"He in turn told me he had been without much sleep the past week because he had been cut from the first-string football team and was having a hard time dealing with it. I told him I knew a little how he felt, because one of the cruelest blows to my pride had occurred in high school when two of my girl friends and I had practiced for months to make the cheerleading team, and they had been chosen and I hadn't.

"My son also told me that he studied very hard, but no matter how hard he tried, he could seldom get better than a 'C.'"

"I guess all I'm trying to do," he told his mother, "is try to feel good about myself, and right now it's pretty hard to do."

We all have it in our power to become Rumpelstilt-skins, capable of the magic of taking the straw of misunderstandings and hidden resentments and turning it into the gold of sympathy and caring. It's easier to do when you realize that in a way we are, all of us, the walking wounded, trapped and lonely on a strange planet and carrying injuries that cannot be seen. Like the teenaged boy, we are trying to feel good about ourselves and sometimes having a hard time succeeding at it.

"KEEP IT FRIENDLY"

Don't exhaust yourself with turmoil and upset; tell yourself to speak your truth quietly and clearly, and as far as you can, keep the situation you're in as friendly as possible.

When you're involved in conflict, meditate about it, and just before you end your session, visualize yourself making the generous, open, and friendly gesture. Then tell yourself to "keep it friendly." Each time before you become involved with the person you might have a disagreement with, remind yourself that your orientation is to "keep it friendly."

In an inspiring book called *A Book of Hours*, the author, Elizabeth Yates, says:

> If I take one of the difficult people and mentally give myself to that person, something is bound to happen. By an exercise of the imagination, I picture myself with that person on a desert island waiting for the turn of the tide, or sheltered in a mountain hut while a storm rages. To survive, each one of us must come to the other's aid. In discovering ourselves as we really are, in the urgency that has been forced upon us, we make room for love to happen. Perhaps the secret is that when response is made as if to a behest from God, a way is opened to let love in. Then the miracle: the realization that love *is*. It can be relied upon to do its work as the sun can be relied upon to shine.
>
> One instance, one exercise: and what if this were carried further? What if every day such an effort were made, not with an imagined situation but on the street, in the office, at home?[4]

4. Elizabeth Yates, *A Book of Hours* (New York: Seabury Press, 1976), p. 29.

Program yourself with the "Keep it friendly" message. Make this an automatic response in your dealing with others. You can hardly go wrong.

"I WILL NOT BE VANQUISHED"

This is the message a mother gave herself in connection with the loss of her three sons. There are many situations in life, less hurtful, when you might wish to tell yourself, "I will not be vanquished."

Mrs. A. B. (not her real initials) is a friend of the family and one of the most productive real estate salespersons in Florida. In 1981 and 1982, the bottom fell out of the real estate market nationwide when the prime interest rate and mortgage rates climbed out of sight. Mrs. B. not only had to contend with a soft real estate market but also with several major personal disappointments and problems during this period. Nevertheless, she kept plugging away, day in and day out, seemingly optimistic and happy.

"How do you do it?" I asked her.

"I refuse to be beaten," she told me. "In a way, it's like riding a horse, I guess. If you fall, you have to brush yourself off and climb back on. You simply have to do that if you are going to keep moving. I don't know any alternative."

"I GIVE MYSELF PERMISSION"

You must give yourself permission to hear what you are telling yourself and examine the statements, suggestions, and messages that you give yourself. You may or may not need to give yourself other permissions, depending on how you were raised.

Some people must give themselves *permission to relax*. They were raised to believe they must be tense and alert to achieve any goal and that grim effort must attend their activities. Often they become workaholics, and while their ability to drive themselves unmercifully may have been the cause of their success, this relentless drive must be examined. It may no longer serve them. They may also need to give themselves *permission to enjoy* what they have accomplished. They may need to take better care of themselves so they will not be the most successful person in the cemetery. It's difficult for these driven people to realize they may lead a balanced life and still experience success beyond their dreams. They need to tell themselves the *whole* truth, and when they do, they will often find that their success was brought about not by their snap and jerk, impatience, tension, eyes on the clock, but in spite of it. During their Creative Meditation sessions they can picture themselves relaxing as they go about their business, working quietly and effectively, doing one thing at a time, becoming goal oriented and not clock oriented. And then, just before they end their session, they can give themselves a powerful permission to stay loose and relaxed as they go about their work.

There are some who need to give themselves *permission to think*. There are those who tell themselves that the way to respond to most problems is to become either emotional, worried, or confused. Like the old joke, "When in danger or in doubt, run in circles, scream and shout."

Jerome Bruner of Harvard states:

There is a sharp distinction that must be made between behavior that *copes* with the requirements of a problem and behavior that is designed to *defend* against entry into the problem. It is the distinction one might make between playing tennis on the one hand and fighting like fury to stay off the tennis court altogether on the other. The latter is not a distorted version of the former; it is different activity, governed by a different objective and different requirements.[5] [Italics are Bruner's.]

In other words, there is a great deal of difference between thinking about a problem and generating all kinds of distractions, such as worry, anger, emotionalism, alcohol, confusion, to avoid confronting the problem, and then acting as if the problem is insoluble and giving up. We must always remember that man is indeed a problem-solving animal and that we must from time to time give ourselves permission to enter the problem and quietly look around—analyze, scan, weigh, balance, compute, play with answers, be tentative, perhaps have a calm discussion with others. (I'll discuss in a later chapter how to use Creative Meditation to help you solve problems, but we must first give ourselves permission to *think* about it.)

Sometimes we must give ourselves a very basic permission; the *permission to be ourselves*. Not everyone has this problem, but more do than you might realize. Some have an idealized image so lofty and unrealistic they can never come close to achieving it. Others waste a lifetime trying to live up to the expectations of other people; then there are those who strive mightily to win the approval, love, or envy of others. They go through life like Sisyphus, never quite succeeding in pushing the boulder to the top of the mountain, never learning one of life's most important lessons: that others can never give you self-esteem; in the end it is a gift you must bestow on yourself. In their Creative Meditation sessions these people need to ask what they are telling themselves that causes them to lose their real live center of being. Before they end their session, they need to tell themselves they will move out from under un-

5. Jerome S. Bruner, *Toward a Theory of Instruction* (New York: W. W. Norton & Company, Inc., 1966), pp. 3–4; reprinted by permission of Harvard University Press, Cambridge, Mass.

realistic expectations, that they will bestow on themselves self-approval; they must give themselves *permission to be themselves*. Emerson expressed it this way:

> My life is for myself and not for a spectacle. I much prefer that it be of a lower strain, so it be genuine and equal, than that it should be glittering and unsteady... Few and mean as my gifts may be, I actually am, and do not need for my own assurance or the assurance of my fellows any secondary testimony. What I must do is all that concerns me, not what the people think.

There are others who must give themselves *permission to be less critical* of themselves and others. They must tell themselves that most of us are doing just about as well as we can under the circumstances and all things considered. As you end your session, if you give yourself just this one permission, to be less critical, you will improve your life greatly; or to program this idea positively, give yourself permission to enjoy others and accept them as they are.

Finally, there are those who must give themselves *permission to live*, to enjoy their hours and days. Not everyone has given himself this permission.

A twenty-nine-year-old acquaintance of mine told me that when he was in college he had sentenced himself to die; he started drinking heavily and steadily, morning, noon, and night. He quit college, moved to Colorado, and waited tables at a restaurant while he relentlessly continued to destroy himself. He then attended three meetings of Alcoholics Anonymous, and one day he made the decision to live. To use his words, "I suddenly, or perhaps not so suddenly, realized that I had condemned myself to death, that I had decided not to live."

When he realized this, he gave himself permission

to listen to his inner conversation; he gave himself permission to live. He told himself he needed help, joined AA, quit drinking, and is making a remarkable comeback.

Many people, not just alcoholics, have not given themselves permission to enjoy life. Supercritical people don't really enjoy life; neither do the workaholics, nor those mired in the victim role, nor the perfectionists, nor the grumblers.

"I'M IN CHARGE OF MY FEELINGS"

Most of us, from time to time, allow others to set our mood. It's sort of silly to say to someone, "You spoiled my day," or, "You made me lose my temper," but we do it. This means that others have the power to decide how we will feel and that we no longer control ourselves. There's no doubt that someone you are close to, or perhaps live with, is going to influence how you feel, at least once in a while. But even here you should keep control of your feelings as much as you possibly can. There are some people who are so sensitive and so little in control of their feelings that they feel rejected if a stranger in an elevator is unfriendly.

Creative Meditation can help you gain control of your feelings so that you have options in your life and don't need to respond to another person's "invitation" to feel bad. In your Creative Meditation session you can visualize yourself remaining calm and in control in a situation that would usually trigger a reaction of bad feelings on your part, repeating over and over, "I'm in charge of my feelings."

Also, in your Creative Meditation session ask what you are telling yourself to cause you to feel a certain way. For example, very often we'll tell ourselves that the other person is deliberately trying to make us angry without ever once thinking how highly improbable that is. You might also wish to ask yourself if you are a "face reader." Do you look at another's face and, from your scrutiny, think you can tell what the other person is thinking and what they are feeling? Nine times out of ten, face readers are wrong. They may think another person is annoyed when the person is merely tired; they may think he is angry when he's really puzzled; they may think he's defiant when he really wants to settle the issue peacefully. Very often people who were raised in a strict household learned at an early age to read the slightest nuance in facial expressions. It was an early warning system that trouble was afoot. They still, years later, see danger or disapproval in faces, often when the other person is not thinking about them at all.

Perhaps you will be able to make a powerful decision and all at once cut the strings that others hold on your emotions. But if you can't do this, you can at least move in that direction so that as you progress, fewer people will hold fewer strings that control your feelings. Believe me, the first time you decline an invitation to feel bad from someone who has heretofore controlled your feelings, you'll find it an exhilarating experience.

"I CHOOSE FREEDOM"

In your Creative Meditation session visualize yourself as a free person, free from all self-criticism, free from all role playing and false fronts. Picture yourself free of the need to seek approval from others, with no need to meet their expectations. Draw up a mental picture of total self-acceptance; feel good all over with the self-esteem you are bestowing upon yourself. Note how good it feels to be free of the need to have the approval of others and how good it feels to have your happiness not dependent on others pleasing you.

In your session recreate your happy and productive moments; relive them, tell yourself about them in detail, stretch them out and inspirit yourself. Think how you can increase the good moments in your life. Tell yourself you are going to move toward goals that are important to you, create more self-actualizing moments, grow toward your potential.

Tell yourself that you are free—free of all the negative feelings, free of the shackles and unnecessary restrictions you have placed on your life. Suffuse yourself with the wonderful feeling of not judging and not being judged, not being critical and not being criticized, totally accepting.

When you are walking around during the day, pause every once in a while and recreate that feeling of freedom.

"I BELIEVE"

This inspiriting Positive Programming message can only be used by those who have a faith, but if you do have one, strong or shaky, it's a good message to give yourself many times during the day and also during your Creative Meditation sessions. As Brother Lawrence said over three hundred years ago:

It is not necessary for being with God to be always at church. We may make an oratory of our heart wherein to retire from time to time to converse with Him in meekness, humility, and love. Everyone is capable of such familiar conversation with God, some more, some less. He knows what we can do. Let us begin, then.[6]

For those who believe that, in C. S. Lewis's words, there is "Something Beyond," then repeating the sim-

6. Brother Lawrence, translated from the French, *The Practice of the Presence of God* (Old Tappan, N.J.: Fleming H. Revell Co., 1958), pp. 48–49.

ple message, "I believe" will be a great help to you. One of the problems for those with faith is that at times there are dark moments of the soul. Not all people with faith suffer these doubts, but many do; even some of the saints did. I think it was St. Francis who said, "Lord, I believe; help Thou mine unbelief."

When you have a strong belief, you have put it together in your mind just right, and it makes sense to you. It appeals to something very deep in your nature, and it's the only key that unlocks the riddle of life itself and the phenomenon of unlikely human creatures on a very strange planet. You think that it's absurd that life would not have a meaning, that someday, when the planet Earth and all of the earthly activity that has gone on for millennia disappear, it will all be as if it had never been. But then, every once in a while, not too often and for no apparent reason, you feel as if it's just as improbable that there would be "Something Beyond"; you feel empty and alone.

What you must remember when this happens is that you don't *always* feel what you *usually* feel. Say you're depressed, exhausted, you've had a discouraging setback, you're sick, or whatever, you start giving yourself a few bad messages that are alien to your nature, and your faith temporarily flies out the window. It is during these times that you should give yourself the message "I believe" over and over to remind yourself of the commitment you have made when you were more yourself. This message will open your mind, and you will remember that you have forgotten.

"I CAN DO IT"

In a poll taken of older people, who were asked what they would do differently if they had it to do all over again, over 85 percent of those surveyed said that if they had their lives to live again, they would take more risks, try more things, dare more. Person after person said that he or she had been too fearful, too afraid of the unknown, and that from their vantage point of years, they can now see there was not that much to fear.

"I can do it." A simple little message, but drum it into your head. I don't mean anyone can be president of the United States; I don't belong to the school of thought that says you can be anything you want. We all have limitations and restrictions, and it's mentally healthy to acknowledge them.

But we don't have nearly as many as we think we do, and it is true that many of us do not take the risks necessary to realize our full potential. You may not be able to be president (or maybe you could be), but you can do much more than you have probably told yourself you can do.

When you're in your Creative Meditation session, visualize yourself doing something you have always wanted to do. Picture it in detail. Then tell yourself, "I can do it." Repeat this to yourself during the day.

Naturally, don't use the "I can do it" message in place of making plans. Always give yourself permission to think and plan in detail. But once your plans are thought out, use this message of "I can do it" to start you on your way and to keep you going over the inevitable rough spots.

The "I can do it" message can remind you that you have the energy to accomplish your goals. Many people don't reach for a goal because they think they don't have the inner resources to see it through. But if you start toward your goal and it becomes interesting to you, then you will have the energy. We all have untapped resources. In your Creative Meditation session, visualize yourself reaching your goal, tell yourself you will enjoy working toward it, that you will have the persistence to stay with it and bountiful energy to achieve it.

Whatever you do, don't tell yourself that you can't do something because you are too old (unless, of course, it's beyond your physical capability). A long time ago, a student told me he didn't want to go on for an advanced degree because when he got it in four years, he would be thirty-five years old. I asked him how old he would be in four years if he didn't go after the degree.

Always tell yourself that what you are living now is the "good old days." They are, you know. You will look back ten years from now, or less, and think of them that way. I think it was Oliver Wendell Holmes who, in his eighties, passed a pretty girl on the street and said, "Oh, to be seventy again."

Tell yourself you can do it and start now. Shakespeare wasn't speaking about time or the value of the present moment, but he could have been when he said:

> What we have we prize not to the worth,
> Whiles we enjoy it; but being lack'd and lost,
> Why then we rack the value; then we find
> The virtue, that possession would not show us
> While it was ours.

"I LIKE MYSELF"

Love for oneself is the foundation of a brotherly society and personal peace of mind.[7]

When the commandment (to love one's neighbor) is rightly understood, it also says the converse, "Thou shall love thyself in the right way."[8]

You find it in book after book: You must like your-

7. Joshua Liebman, *Peace of Mind* (New York: Simon and Schuster, 1955).
8. Sören Kierkegaard, *Works of Love*, trans. David Swenson (New York: Harper and Row, 1962).

self. You have no choice if you wish to be happy. In fact, most of those who write on the subject go further and say that you must love yourself. They don't mean, of course, that you should pamper or glorify yourself or be steeped in vain conceit; they mean that you and I, with humility, must be aware of our limitations and strengths and respect ourselves, give ourselves a high rating.

I think most of us know already that to have any kind of life at all, we must respect and like ourselves. It's a psychological cliché. The trouble comes about because we know it on an intellectual level but don't make it a part of our daily lives. We don't internalize it.

The admonition to love yourself is not only a psychological truth but one of the cornerstones of the Judeo-Christian religion, one of the Ten Commandments: love thy neighbor as thyself. You are commanded to love your neighbor *and* yourself because if you don't love yourself, there is no way you can love your neighbor. Some theologians substitute the word "respect" for "love," but it still holds true that you must respect yourself if you are to respect your neighbor.

What we often do after reading that we must like ourselves is nod our heads wisely—after all, who doesn't know that if they constantly downgrade themselves they are bound to be unhappy—then go right back to our self-rejecting ways.

If you choose "I Like Myself" as one of your Positive Programming messages, you must repeat it to yourself many times during the day. Just once or twice won't do it.

We can take the first step toward self-acceptance by saying to our souls, "I have difficulty in accepting myself but God accepts me, and I will accept myself." We may need to make this prayer of affirmation numberless times before we succeed in counteracting the effects of years of self-rejection.[9]

The last sentence in the above quote bears repeating: "We may need to make this prayer of affirmation numberless times before we succeed in counteracting the effects of years of self-rejection." Positive Programming is based on well-tested learning theory that the more you repeat an idea, the better you remember it and the more it becomes a part of you. Repeat to yourself, as in the above quote, for example, "God accepts me, and I accept myself" in your full Creative Meditation sessions and many times a day in your instant Creative Meditation sessions, and after three or four months of doing this, you will have programmed yourself in a positive way to accept yourself. If you find comfort in the message "God accepts me and I accept myself" and repeat it only a few times, the thought will not stay with you or become part of your subconscious.

In your Creative Meditation session you might wish to role play and pretend you are a consultant and have yourself for a client. What changes would you advise? Perhaps let up a little? Enjoy yourself a little more? Be less critical of yourself and others? Give up your perfectionistic demands? Learn to shrug your shoulders more often and let events roll off your back? Stop thinking you are the victim of injustice? Write out a prescription for yourself, much as a doctor would prescribe a drug, and then follow your orders and see if you don't become a little happier.

You can Positive Program yourself by repeating many times per day, "I like myself." You may already

9. Taken from *The Art of Understanding Yourself*, by Cecil Osborne. Copyright © 1967 by Zondervan Publishing House. Used by permission. (p. 217.)

be programmed by yourself and others to put yourself down, give yourself a low rating, so that what you're really doing is taking charge of yourself and programming yourself the way *you* decide. During the day you may wish to "listen in" to what you tell yourself and see if you have subtle ways of putting yourself down. Bring those negative messages out in the open and then counteract them with your message of "I like myself" or "You're doing a fine job, all things considered." Here's what Carl Rogers said about enjoying and liking yourself:

> . . . So I let go of all responsibility except the responsibility—and the satisfaction—of being myself. For me it was a most unusual feeling: to be comfortably irresponsible with no feeling of guilt. And, to my surprise, I found I was more effective that way.
>
> I have taken better care of myself physically, in a variety of ways. I have also learned to respect my psychological needs. Three years ago a workshop group helped me to realize how harried and driven I felt by outside demands—'nibbled to death by ducks' was the way one person put it, and the expression captured my feelings exactly. So I did what I have never done before: I spent ten days absolutely alone in a beach cottage which had been offered me and I refreshed myself immensely; I found I thoroughly enjoyed being with me. I *like* me.[10]

During your Creative Meditation session to explore the depth and quality of your self-esteem, you may wish to ask yourself some of the following questions:

- Do I have inner tyrants that keep me down? Do I accept myself? Am I comfortable with myself,

10. Carl R. Rogers: *A Way of Being*, Copyright © 1981 Houghton Mifflin Company. Used by permission.

or do my inner tyrants keep me from enjoying life to the fullest possible? Are they constantly dissatisfied, driving me to do more and more with no rest? Do they keep me tense and hurried, always fighting the clock? Do they keep me tense with the feeling of effort? Do they demand perfection?

• Do I nurture myself? Do I take good care of my mind and body? Am I careful what I tell myself about myself? Do I control my thoughts, or do I, for example, keep putting myself down, filling my mind with discouraging ideas?

• Do I realize that mental health requires that I like myself? Do I realize that in some ways my mind is like a computer and that the aphorism about computers applies to my mind: garbage in, garbage out. Do I give myself hopeful messages or despairing ones? Someone once remarked to Winston Churchill that he noticed he was always optimistic, to which Churchill replied, "I see no point in being otherwise."

• Do I lead a conditional life? Do I like myself only *if*: if I am brighter, smarter, faster, better-looking, more important, richer than others? A conditional life is a precarious one at best, because sooner or later you will not be able to meet your demands for perfection, or you will make a mistake, or you will not be able to outstrip your rivals, and then you will sentence yourself to what Eric Berne calls your "favorite miserable feeling." This is the feeling you habitually throw yourself into when you condemn yourself for not achieving what is usually an unrealistic goal.

• Are my goals realistic? Several studies have proven that people who have a high need for achievement set *moderate* goals. I'm aware of what you might be thinking, because whenever I bring this up in class, many of the students, whether they are undergraduates, graduate students, or experienced businessmen and women, doubt this statement; haven't they always been told they should aim high, shoot for the moon? Well, doubt it or not, it's true, and for a very basic reason. Other studies show that success breeds success. In other words, "nothing succeeds like success," and one good way to experience success is to set moderate goals, goals that are possible to reach so that you are not constantly frustrating yourself. Don't sit down to write a book, the very thought is overwhelming; set a goal of one good page a day. And at the end of a year or so you'll have your book. I forget who first said this—it sure wasn't Shakespeare—but it still expresses very well what I'm saying: "By the yard, life is hard. By the inch, life's a cinch."

• Do I torture myself because I have too many "shoulds" and "oughts" in my life? Do you, for example, think you should always place other's wishes ahead of your own, should never argue with your spouse, should never be angry with your children, should always be brilliant or cheerful or wise or perfect? Should, should, should—never-ending demands on yourself for a performance impossible for a mere human being to achieve.

• Am I a problem to myself? This is a good question to ask yourself every once in a while during your Creative Meditation session. Ask yourself how many of your difficulties are self-inflicted, how much trouble you bring on yourself. Wouldn't you be happier and more effective if you didn't become discouraged or offended or frustrated or guilt ridden quite so often? If your negative feelings are habitual, you can program a Positive Programming reaction to come between the stimulus and your old way of responding.

Repeat, Repeat, Repeat

You must repeat many times during the day whatever Positive Programming message you choose. Make it a litany (I sometimes refer to it as a mantra) that you say over and over to yourself when in your Creative Meditation session and as you are going about your business at home or work. When you sense that you are going into your old practiced feeling of anger, guilt, unhappiness, hurt, impatience, inferiority, inadequacy, worry, confusion, joylessness, hopelessness, discouragement, whatever, then cut in with your Positive Programming message over and over and over. Doing this, you are training both your conscious and subconscious mind.

The repetition is essential. Remember, you are trying to form a new habit; you're actually making a behavioral change, one that you have decided to make so that your response to life will fit your predominant theme, your real self, and you must repeat this new response until it becomes automatic and extinguishes your old response. Give the new message to yourself first thing in the morning, throughout your day, and then at night before you go to sleep.

You're breaking some lifelong habits, and it will not happen overnight. But keep at it and enjoy it. Just think, you are taking an active role in creating for yourself peace, happiness, calmness, and effectiveness. When you program yourself positively, you are putting yourself in charge; you are the one who decides what your response will be.

Don't forget. Repeat . . . repeat . . . repeat.

VI

What Do You Ask Yourself in Your Creative Meditation Session?

... a man is continually revolting against an *effect* without, while all the time he is nourishing and preserving its *cause* in his heart.

James Allen

To have a good life, you must have good hours.
Ancient wisdom

In your Creative Meditation session, whether you're conversing with yourself or your "wise friend," the conversation can be the same. Remember, it's your session, and you can talk about what you want, but your questions must be nonaggressive and nondemanding. Here are a few sample questions, some you may want to ask, some you'll not be interested in. I would advise you, especially at the beginning, to work on only one area per session. If you're upset and nervous, identify the messages you give yourself to cause that feeling and don't work on anything else. Remember, one of your goals is to find out what you are telling yourself, another is to discover the truth in a situation, and a third goal is to program yourself positively. For example, you might wish to ask:

Why was I angry?
Why was I hurt?
Why was I prideful?
Why was I nervous?
Why did I feel humiliated?
Why am I fearful?
Why did I feel inferior?

And always quietly ask, "What am I *telling myself* to cause my anger, hurt, nervousness, humiliation, fear, etc.?" Ask, "What messages, statements, suggestions do I give myself to cause these feelings? Are they true?"

If you're angry, for example, don't meet it head-on. After all, you've fought that bad habit for the thousandth time and haven't conquered it. William James said to resist a bad habit merely adds force to it by focusing attention on it. And remember I said earlier that a habit effectively blocks all other responses. In other words, your anger habit keeps you from responding to certain situations any other way. So what can you do?

When you're angry, ask what you are telling yourself to cause your anger. If the answer is that it's because one of your children or your spouse or friend hurt your feelings (anger is often caused by hurt feelings), then don't stop there. Ask yourself what is the whole truth about the situation or about the other person. Remember the good times. Remind yourself of the other side of the person, the good side.

And always seek a *precise* definition for the cause of your hurt or anger. Say to yourself, "I'm hurt because ————." (You fill in the blank.)

If you're angry (and hurt) because someone didn't help you or forgot your birthday or ignored advice or contradicted you or slighted you in some way, tell yourself the *whole* truth about the situation, forgive the person even for the hundredth time, if forgiveness is called for, and make an adult decision to repeat your Positive Programming message over and over: "It is not '*unfair*,' it just '*is*,'" or, "I choose happiness," or, "Keep it friendly," or, "Straw into gold."

In your Creative Meditation session you might wish to explore some of the following areas:

• Do I feel critical or disapproving of myself or others? How have I become that way? What are the messages, statements, suggestions I give myself that cause this? Are they true? Do they help me?

• What are the long-term goals that are important to me? Will my near-term goals help me reach my long-term goals? If I go on as I am, will I reach my goals?

• What are the really happy moments in my life? What do I really enjoy? Can I increase my happy moments?

• What do I tell myself about: money, work, sex, health, love, parenting, authority, religion, life after death, my energy level, friends, my parents, my children? Are the statements I tell myself about these subjects the truth and the whole truth? How can I change the statements to make myself happier? How can I change the claims and expectations I have to give myself greater peace of mind?

• What do I consider really important in my relations with those I love? What do I tell myself about those I love?

• What are my "how to's"? Do I cause myself and others unhappiness because I have told myself there are strict rules on how to:

celebrate holidays
show love
run a house
relate to one another
make love
show affection
spend leisure time
gain respect
get things done

• Do I have inner tyrants who drive me unmercifully? Do I "try hard," teeth clenched, body tense, serious, firm of purpose, anxious, rather than just relaxing and doing?

• Am I perfectionistic, never letting go, never allowing myself and others just to do well and not be perfect? Do I sometimes feel flooded with hopelessness because I can't reach perfection? Is this productive?

• Do I insist that others do things my way, cater to me, be attentive to my whims; or, conversely, is there someone I'm always trying to please?

• Am I always in a hurry, rushing, feeling pressed and behind? Can I set a more relaxed, comfortable pace and get as much done?

• What are the inner statements and messages I tell myself to cause my inner tyrants to drive me on? Do I really want to live this way? Can I take charge?

• Do I have a role I play that is unproductive? Am I, for example, often a "victim"? Do I walk around feeling hurt? What do I tell myself that causes this feeling? Are there better feelings than hurt? What do I tell myself I should expect of others? Are my expectations realistic? Do I purposely set myself up for this feeling? Is it a racket feeling or does it have a legitimate purpose? Will the role of victim bring me the happiness I want, or is it a habit?

• Is my role that of 24-hour on-duty police officer, always regulating, laying down rules, strict, enforcing, catching family or friends breaking the rules, exposing violations, berating? What am I telling myself that causes me to do this? Will things really go to pieces if I take it a little easy? Am I really the only conscientious person around? What do I tell myself that causes me to act this way?

• Do I play the role of Johnny or Mary to the rescue? Always on the spot to clear up trouble, smooth out conflict, keep the peace, come to the aid of the "victim"? Do I really need to volunteer as much? Am I always trying to make peace while, sometimes, perhaps, fanning the flames? What do I tell myself that causes me to help even when it's not needed or wanted?

• Do I allow myself and those I love to live fully, to enjoy life, to think in depth about everything, to be what we are, to get close?

• How can I get the most out of today? How can I enjoy today? How can I go for the good feelings? What do I need to avoid? What will be the good moments? Can I stretch them? What do I need to tell myself that will bring me happiness today? If I tell myself I'm a victim or tell myself someone needs to be controlled, corrected, or rescued, what feelings will these statements lead to? Are these the feelings I want?

Don't Be Critical

The above questions are to get you started. Many of them may not apply to you. You may have areas you wish to explore that are not covered above; by all means, do so. The session is yours to do with as you wish. There are several simple rules to follow, however. First, do not be critical or judgmental. Your objective is to explore and examine, to find out what you're telling yourself, to search for truth. Second, only cover one area per session and keep coming back to that. Third, give yourself only positive and life-giving messages, statements, and suggestions while in this state of relaxation.

Make Only Positive Suggestions

Remember this about Creative Meditation and Positive Programming: During your session, you can give yourself messages and suggestions that will be with you and "bubble up" later as you go about your business. That's why you must give yourself only positive, uplifting, nurturing, and hopeful suggestions during the session. Plant these forceful messages in your brain where they will keep working for you. Tell yourself, for example, how well you are doing, congratulate yourself or tell yourself how well you'll feel and all the energy you'll have, or plant the message that you are going to take charge of your life, free of your inner tyrant.

During the session, if you wish, allow your "wise friend" to tell you nurturing and positive things about yourself. Set positive goals and visualize them. If you want to stop smoking or lose weight, tell yourself the positive benefits; picture yourself as you will look and feel when you reach your goals; plant the message that when you want a cigarette or a snack you'll stop and meditate for a minute or two. Once again, be certain to tell yourself how calm, peaceful, and joyous you are going to feel when you end your session. These inner messages will rise from your unconscious as your day unfolds, and you will find, from time to time, a mysterious and unexplained sense of well-being, a timed-release effect.

Relax, It's Your Session

Your interest in a book such as this indicates that you're a conscientious person. If you're like many of us, you may be over-conscientious. Perhaps just a little bit perfectionistic.

Please don't carry this perfectionism to your Creative Meditation sessions. Don't wonder constantly if you're doing it right, if you have done it long enough, if you have relaxed as much as you should have, if you have asked the right questions.

Remember this about perfectionism, whether it's in Creative Meditation or any other endeavor. You only fail at something when you quit trying; if you try to do something perfectly, the chances are you will become tense and hopeless and quit. Relax. Easy does it!

Speaking of perfectionism reminds me of a session with a group of men and women during which I carefully went over each point in this chapter and then repeated them. We then had a practice Creative Meditation session, after which I answered questions. At the end of the session a man came up to me and said, "Nelson, that was great. My wife and I both got a lot out of it. We intend to continue doing it just as soon as we learn how!"

"What do you mean when you learn how?" I asked him. "You already know how. I covered all the points with you."

"We want to get it just right," he said.

The answer to this man and to others who may have doubts is that this chapter and others show you how to do it and, really, you were born with the ability to relax, meditate, and tune in on yourself. Use the suggestions in this book, improvise a little to suit your own life-style and problems, and you'll be doing fine. The question to ask yourself is not whether you are doing it perfectly but are you feeling better, able to control yourself more, relieve your stress, experience more peace of mind and happiness.

Some of your sessions will be better than others. You may relax more, perhaps program positive new "pathways" in your mind. These sessions will seem to you to be more productive. Another session, perhaps only lasting a minute because you cannot spare more time, may give you an insight, help you untangle a knotty problem, or maybe just furnish you with an island during stress. They will all be different, but you will benefit from each and every session.

But please don't try for a perfect session. Don't "try hard." When you think about it, one of our goals during a Creative Meditation session is to relax completely and let go as much as possible, and we're not going to do that if we constantly monitor ourselves to see how well we are doing. If, for example, you are talking with your "wise friend," your visualization of him or her will fade in and out. You'll get some answers, on some questions you'll draw a blank, there will be periods of silence, or maybe nothing but silence, and then an answer will pop into your consciousness later in the day. In your session you may visualize future goals, see yourself responding in a positive way to situations that used to cause you discomfort, imagine yourself with a new good habit in place of an undesirable one, give yourself encouraging suggestions. Don't structure it too much, don't be rigid, and remember to repeat your Positive Programming message over and over.

Instant Creative Meditation Sessions

After you practice Creative Meditation for a few weeks, you will be able to achieve a state of relaxation in a few seconds. To help you accomplish this, during your longer sessions you can plant the message in your mind that all you need do is give yourself the "Light Touch" cue.

I said that the ideal length of time, for many, to practice Creative Meditation is ten to twenty minutes. However, when you become adept at achieving relaxation in a short time, you can then practice Creative Meditation sessions for periods even shorter than a minute. Instant Creative Meditation sessions are just like regular sessions except they are shorter. They can last from several seconds to several minutes, and you can go through the same processes you do in a regular session of longer duration.

Two Creative Meditation sessions per day lasting ten to twenty minutes each would give you the most benefits. That would be ideal. But most people won't do this *even if they know it will benefit them greatly*. They either don't have the time or do not want to sit still that long every day. Records kept on those who practiced passive meditation show the dropout rate is extremely high. Although Creative Meditation is different from most forms of meditation in that you are not striving for a mindless state but engaged in more interesting work during your session, I know that many of you will not keep at it for twenty or thirty minutes each and every day.

If you can't or won't spend that long each day, then have as many instant sessions as you can. Relax and tune in on your inner dialogue, find out what you're telling yourself, and give yourself your Positive Programming message(s). This will only take several seconds to several minutes and will still bring you benefits. This will also keep you in touch with Creative Meditation so that you will be familiar with it and have it at your disposal during periods of unusual stress and conflict when you will want your sessions to be longer.

As I write this, I'm reminded of the story told by William James about the man who found himself at night slipping down the side of a precipice. At last the man caught a branch, which stopped his fall, and he remained clinging to it in misery for hours. But finally his fingers had to loose their hold, and with a despairing farewell to life, he let himself drop. He fell just six inches! You, too, may be hanging on for dear life when the best thing you could do for yourself would be to relax and let go.

You can use instant Creative Meditation almost anytime: just before an important meeting, interview, luncheon engagement, speech, or conference with your boss, before the kids come home, after an argument, or even during one, or just to give yourself an interval of peace and relaxation and your Positive Programming message.

You can also use it the same as you do your full-length session to find out what you are telling yourself that causes you to feel a certain way, or what inner messages are causing you stress and conflict. The instant sessions give you instant rewards and a chance to "let go."

VII

Your Unconscious Hidden Messages

Everything begins with awareness.
Frederick Perls

A close friend confessed to me one day that she had originally thought Positive Programming was similar to brainwashing. "I like to be spontaneous," she said, "and not tied down to the same ideas day after day."

I told this woman that Positive Programming is nothing like brainwashing, that what it does, in effect, is counteract the *unconscious* brainwashing that's been done. It makes you the active agent and helps you become spontaneous and get in touch with yourself.

The comment on Positive Programming was odd coming from this woman. I knew her well enough to tell her that her life was filled with unconscious programming. One of her inner commands, driving her on, was, "Be neat ... at all costs." Her family was not allowed in the living room, as they might mess it up. Every room was scrubbed and immaculate. Because of constant criticism, one of her sons moved out of the house. He told her at the time that the atmosphere in the house was too tense and that he couldn't take her constant criticism of his ways.

Her husband had one chair assigned to him and even then had to cover it with a large bath towel before he sat in it.

This woman was a good enough friend that, without getting angry, she allowed me to point out some of her unconscious or barely conscious habits. In addition to her "be neat no matter what the cost in family happiness," she was very critical of herself as well as the members of her family. I told her she was so burdened with her unending attention to every detail of living, in her own life and in the lives of every member of her family, that she didn't get much joy from life and kept others from it, too. To her, life was a problem and not a privilege. I suggested she think about this and perhaps use as her Positive Programming message, "I Choose Happiness." (See chapter V on Positive Programming.)

If she asked, during her Creative Meditation sessions, what she was telling herself, the statements and messages behind her "Be neat" drive, and then many times during the day repeated her "I Choose Happiness" mantra, she might be able to give herself and her family more joy and happiness.

You can be reasonably sure of this: if you are critical of yourself, you will be critical of others; if you demand perfection from yourself, you will demand it of others. These two traits alone, programmed in us at an early age, can cause a great deal of unhappiness. I know it's easy to say you should stop being critical and perfectionistic but that it's difficult to accomplish. But you can do it if you program yourself positively with a life-enriching message and repeat it whenever your inner tyrants take over. When you criticize yourself or someone else, cut in with your life-giving message; cut your inner tyrant short. With members of your family you may even wish to apologize. Pick out a Positive Programming message that will work for you or make up one yourself.

There are many examples of unconscious, or barely conscious, programming that keep us from becoming a fully functioning human being. The list of short statements in the first chapter furnishes examples of programming that limit our lives unnecessarily. There is hardly an hour during the day when we aren't being bombarded with suggestions and messages. As I said earlier, we are programmed by our parents, our teachers, our friends (and some of this is good programming), and by television and other media. Often, without knowing it, we react to these suggestions, and some of them become a part of us.

Permission to Become Aware

Many years ago Socrates said that an unexamined life is not worth living. This still holds true today. And, of course, that's what we are talking about in this book—using Creative Meditation to discover how we are conditioned by others and by what we are telling ourselves, ridding ourselves of negative messages, then programming a positive message and repeating it so that it becomes part of us.

Fritz Perls said that everything begins with awareness. One of the quickest and most interesting ways to greatly improve your life is to become aware of your inner communication. You listen to yourself and catch yourself on the wing, so to speak.

The Hidden Message Is "Be Scared"

A father told me that one day his eighteen-year-old son pulled him up short when he said, "Dad, why are you always so negative? I don't want to go through life feeling that way. I've got to be confident and hopeful if I'm going to do anything."

The father continued:

> At first I couldn't believe what I was hearing. All my life I had been optimistic, taking one chance after another, pretty sure everything would come out all right, and here was my son telling me I was always so negative. Then I got thinking about what he said. Ninety percent of my conversation with him consisted of warning him about the pitfalls in life, the dangers, the down cycles; what to watch out for, what to avoid, how to be careful. I tuned into my inner conversation, and although I have been blessed most of my life, I had become very negative. My conversation with my family was sprinkled with warnings. I had even started giving out negative advice I didn't really believe in myself. In effect, since you have to live life, anyway, and since it's almost impossible to prepare people for all the events they are going to live through, my major message to them was, "Be scared."

As you become aware of some of the statements you make, both to yourself and others, gradually cut down on the negative, life-restricting, joy-reducing messages. In spewing forth negative messages, you not only poison the lives of others and foist your distortions on them, such as that father did, but you yourself hear what you're saying and believe it. You mesmerize yourself.

The Hidden Message Is "Don't Enjoy Life"

Last fall I sat next to a stranger as we were riding the monorail to the Epcot Center in Disney World.

"I'm not going to like this at all," said the man. "I'm just going because I live close by in Orlando."

"Have you been there before?" I asked.

"Nope, first time," he said.

"What makes you think you're not going to like it?"

"I don't know," he answered. "I don't think it's going to be interesting."

By accident I ran into this same man getting off the Showcase to the World ride forty-five minutes later. The ride was interesting and just scary enough to be thrilling.

"How did you like the ride?" I asked him.

"Just what I thought," he answered. "There's nothing to it."

He walked away in the direction of the next ride, shaking his head, doggedly going about his strange mission. Give yourself negative messages and you'll come to the conclusion—whether it's about a billion dollar investment in Florida that you've paid good money to see, or about your own life—that, "There's nothing to it."

Listen to your own conversation and realize what effect you have on your own happiness. Unbalanced, discouraging, negative messages and suggestions poison your mind; they are real and have a real effect on your life.

Patterns and Pathways

Much of what we have programmed in us is desirable and essential. Our inner messages, attitudes, reactions, must, to a great extent, be automatic, or we couldn't function. By being automatic, they also make us dependable and reliable, and there is little doubt that this is a worthwhile goal.

But there are times when we would rather have options than react automatically. In other words, we would like to have the option of not reacting to a certain event in the same way each time. When someone cuts us off in traffic, we experience freedom if we don't have to react with anger. The sad thing about the driver who gives you the finger is not so much that he is rude but that his reactions are so limited and unoriginal.

Other examples of automatic programmed response abound. We try to give the child advice, he reacts with a deep sigh, an upward, despairing roll of the eyes seeking divine help in dealing with yet another example of our unreasonableness, and we then blow our top. The boss frowns, and we feel fear. The spouse takes position A, we make our predictable response of C, and the fight is on. Or perhaps we just read in the paper about someone who appears luckier, younger, richer, or whatever than we are, and we feel down.

Psychologists have various names for these predictable reactions. When I was writing about transactional analysis, I liked the words Eric Berne used. He said that we had "tapes" in our heads that played upon certain provocation. These tapes were originally recorded when we were very young; most of them were put there by our parents; they are called parent tapes. Everything we have experienced through our senses is stored in our brain. A neurosurgeon, Wilder Penfield, found that by touching a certain area in the brain, you could cause a person to recreate in full, including sight, sound, and smell, experiences in his youth.

Another way to picture our reactions is to picture a pathway in the brain. As I said before, many of these pathways are beneficial; indeed, we couldn't live without them. We give the mind the initial instruction "Eat breakfast" and then hardly think about it. Our neurons start firing off orders to tendons, muscles, our sense of sight, sound, smell, touch, and hearing, and we can prepare and consume a large breakfast while thinking about a dozen other events. It's all programmed into patterns and pathways.

But so is that anger reaction you have from time to time, or your envy, fear, guilt, shame, or your constant criticism of people and events. The neurons start firing away just as they do when you order yourself to get breakfast. Like a roller coaster at an amusement park, the lever is thrown, and away you go on a predetermined path.

You can use Creative Meditation to change those pathways. When you are in your session, visualize yourself reacting differently. Think about yourself feeling hurt, say, when a member of your family or a friend doesn't, for the thousandth time, seem to want your advice. Don't say to yourself, "I won't get hurt again." That doesn't work, but ask what you are telling yourself to cause these reactions. Is your inner message, for example, "I'm not important," "I'm not respected," "Nobody thinks I know anything," "If I were so and so, I'll bet they would listen"? Find the statements that cause the feelings. Change those inner messages and statements to positive messages, and you'll change the pathways.

Tell yourself that there are better reactions than anger, hurt, shame, or guilt and that you have options. Picture yourself having a different reaction than you usually do. And ask yourself why, in the example above, you would feel hurt when someone doesn't take your advice. Are you telling yourself they don't respect you? That's misinformation, you know.

In this situation as in others, tell yourself the *whole* truth. People don't take your advice not because they don't respect you but because they don't like advice period. It's no wonder; nine times out of ten the advice we get is someone telling us not to do something we want to do or vice versa.

If your reactions are not what you would like them to be, perhaps you should visualize yourself taking things less seriously, with just a little more of a smile and a shrug of the shoulders. Niels Bohr, the famous scientist, was once criticized by a graduate student because he allowed much laughter and levity in his laboratory. He answered the criticism by saying, "There are some things so important you can only joke about them." If you can laugh about important things, you can surely laugh about unimportant ones. Start changing your inner message from "I'm hurt" or "I'm angry" or "I'm humiliated" to "That's humorous" or "That's life" or shrug your shoulders and tell yourself, "It's not important."

When you are in your Creative Meditation session, picture yourself acting in different situations the way you want to act, being what you want yourself to be, in charge, and not reacting negatively to another person or event. In this way, you will erase the old pathways and patterns and implant new ones that will serve you better. Always ask what you are telling yourself to make you feel and react a certain way. And then analyze your inner statement to make sure it is precise, accurate, and represents the truth, the whole truth, and nothing but the truth.

Inner Communication Must Be the Whole *Truth*

All of us must question the truth of our inner communication. Insofar as is humanly possible, for mental health, we must keep our inner messages and suggestions free of distortion and error. As with most things in life, this is easier said than done.

You might wish to read over the list of simple statements at the beginning of this book and add any others that you hear yourself saying. When you're fearful or harbor resentment or feel guilty or have made yourself or others unhappy for any reason—this is the time to pull yourself up short and start questioning the truth of what you are telling yourself. One quick and easy way to do this is to ask yourself: "Is what I am telling myself the whole truth?"

Your guiding principle, always, should be to go for the good feelings. And, of course, since your inner communication determines how you feel, the way to go for the good feelings is to tell yourself the whole truth, free of distortion, and to make your inner communication as life-giving as possible.

In the end, the quality of our life will be determined by the amount of loving kindness we have shown to others and to *ourselves*. (It's a psychological truth that you cannot be kind to others unless you are kind to yourself; or, conversely, if you tyrannize yourself, you will tyrannize others as surely as night follows day. And your tyranny both to yourself and others will be because you don't know how to achieve your objectives or reach your goals any other way.)

Start talking to yourself in specific, definite, and concrete terms and, as much as possible, go for the good feelings. For example, don't say, "I'm no good," or, "I'm always making mistakes," or, "She makes me sick," but state in specific terms what you or the other person did or said and make yourself include all sides of the story.

Develop the habit of talking to yourself in specific, truthful sentences with no distortion. Say the sentence out loud if it helps. Examine what you have said and then make yourself state something hopeful about it; do this, and in time it will become a habit. Think of past problems that disappeared or turned out to be inconsequential. Remember the positive factors at work in those past situations. Wouldn't a balanced analysis have served you better then? How about a balanced, hopeful analysis now?

I'm reminded of an acquaintance who, whenever he was presented with a problem, would say, "Well, good," and then follow it with a bracing remark such as, "It will only take a minute to fix," or, "Well, good, she sure didn't mean to mess up our bank account." When I first heard him doing this and asked him about it, he said, "I had a heart attack several years ago that I'm convinced I brought on myself by always making negative statements, fighting trifles, and looking on the dark side of things. I say, 'Well, good,' because anything is better than another heart attack. Besides, it makes me feel better."

Stop Playing Win/Lose

Don't set up any more win/lose situations in your life than you absolutely have to. If you tell yourself you'll be happy only if you finish project "X" by 3:00 P.M., or if the market goes up, or if you get two new clients, finish three pages, get a bonus, raise outstanding children, whatever, you're setting yourself up for a great deal of unhappiness. You will live a yo-yo life, up and down, filled with unreasonable demands set by yourself and sudden disappointments. Your happiness and peace of mind will be in the hands of a fate you can't control, to be blown about like a feather in the wind. Again, Shakespeare said it well:

> Look, as I blow this feather from my face,
> And as the air blows it to me again,
> Obeying with my wind when I do blow,
> And yielding to another when it blows,
> Commanded always by the greater gust.

Henry VI Part III Act III

Refuse to be commanded by the greater gust, especially in the small, unimportant things in life. Someone once said that there is sickness and death, and everything else is mere events. I don't quite believe that. We can't help wanting to win in many cases and being disappointed if it doesn't work out. But even here, and you know this from experience, so often the opportunity missed turns out in the long run to be unimportant. Looking back on the landscape of life, the hills and valleys tend to flatten out.

Reduce as much as possible the times you tell yourself, "If that happens, I win."

Numbers, Numbers, Numbers

Don't tell yourself that it's the numbers that count most in your life. If they are up, you're up; if they are down, you're down. You can't really quantify your worth as a human being, and you and I really know this. If you tell yourself that what is truly important is the number of square feet in your house, your yearly income, your net worth, the cost of your car, then you're headed for trouble. Many of us tend to do this, and it brings us to all sorts of mischief. Eric Berne said that for many people in our culture the predominant psychological game they play is "Mine is better than yours."

A doctor in a large city in Florida ran his patients through his office like cattle; they were not people but $25 bills. He was curt, unfriendly, full of himself, always overbooked. After all, didn't he have the big house, big car, big bank account? But no one really liked him—not his nurses, his patients, his family; he didn't even like himself. He viewed his patients as numbers and, inevitably, viewed himself merely as a number, whipping in and out of cubicles, trying to rack up more each day, sort of a medical automated Scrooge. We're lucky most doctors are not like that.

Driven people whose inner messages are empty and acquisitive are concerned with what they are achieving in terms of numbers and not with what they are being and becoming. Sure, everyone wants to live as well as he can. Therefore, do it! And be concerned with the *quality* of your life, the humanity in it for yourself and others, and not just with the quantity, the numbers and amounts. Think of the persons in your life whom you respected the most, and the chances are you'll see with blinding clarity your love and respect had little to do with what they had achieved in material goods; it was based on what kind of human beings they were. Deep down you won't respect yourself for such superficial reasons, either.

My crown is in my heart, not on my head,
Not deck'd with diamonds and Indian stones,

Nor to be seen: my crown is called content;
A crown it is that seldom kings enjoy.

Henry VI Part III Act III, Scene 1

Your Expectations Can Defeat You

A residential home builder told me that he expects several things to go wrong each week at his building sites.

Too much lumber will be ordered, the marble sills will be scratched, the wrong color paint will be used, a tile will be cracked, the wallboard will separate, the subcontractor won't show up. It goes with the territory...." He continued, "I used to get upset about it. Then one day I was watching an interview of a professional football coach with one of the best win records in the NFL. When the interviewer asked him how he had felt when his team fumbled, for the second time, during the fourth quarter, the coach answered, "I expect to fumble a certain number of times each year. I don't like it, but it's part of the game." That's what I tell myself now," said the builder. I expect things to go wrong with each house. It's part of the game.

I was talking with another builder, just two months later, who was in despair because, he said, everything was going wrong on an expensive house he was building. It seems the main problems were that the subcontractors were always a day or two behind the date they promised. "Isn't that always the way when houses are selling fast?" I asked him.

"Yeah! Just let business get a little good and they're always behind," he answered.

This man can't win with what he is telling himself.

When business is good, he's constantly upset because his subcontractors fall behind. When business is bad, he's more upset because he can't sell the houses he builds. Just last month this builder had open-heart surgery.

Happiness Equals Accomplishments Minus Unrealistic Expectations

It is not thy duty to finish the work, but thou art not at liberty to neglect it.

... do not say "I shall drive myself excessively in my study, the way workers do who have to finish a fixed task!" For if you act this way you will in the end grow weak and sluggish and cease from the work altogether. He who tries to do more than he is able will in the end do less...

The Living Talmud

If you tell yourself you can get the job done in a day and it takes three days, you'll be unhappy. Your expectations were too unrealistic. If you expect that your day will go smoothly but you experience the usual annoyances, you'll feel frustrated and unhappy.

Effective people do not frustrate themselves. They try to keep their expectations realistic. They know that Murphy's Law, "If anything can go wrong, it will," is alive and working. They know that Murphy was also right with his corollaries: "Nothing is as easy as it looks," and, "Everything takes longer than you think." Don't constantly frustrate yourself with unrealistic expectations.

C. S. Lewis was talking about expectations when he said much of your happiness depends on whether you view the earth as a prison or a hotel. If you view it as a prison, then you'll be pleased at all the extra advantages you have; view it as a hotel, and you will have all sorts of complaints about the service.

Your Claims Cause Unhappiness and Despair

In one of her many helpful books, *Our Inner Conflicts*, Karen Horney says we could be happier if we didn't have so many claims on life. She says many times our claims cause conflicts so great that we become hopeless.

Think for a moment of the claims some of us have. We make claims that those we work with be reasonable and understanding, our spouse be always attentive, we suffer no illness, people show us respect and pay attention to our needs and ideas; we must be top dog, smarter, wiser, richer, better looking, faster thinking, have better taste, etc. than others; also, that people do not interrupt us, that they always agree with us— the list could go on. Take a look at what you tell yourself you may rightfully expect from life and see if your claims are truly reasonable. Remember that your claims are often hidden until you get in touch with your inner communication. If once in a while you have flashes of despair and hopelessness, it could be because your claims on life are so unreasonable, even outlandish, that you despair of reaching them.

Karen Horney uses, as an example of unreasonable claims, the people in Chekhov's *Cherry Orchard*, who are facing bankruptcy and are in despair at the thought of moving away from their estate, with its beloved cherry orchard. Then a man of affairs offers the sound suggestion that they build small houses for rent on a part of their estate. This would solve their problem, and they would not have to move. To them, this is unthinkable; they think they have a "right" not to share their estate with anyone. "It's not right to have to rent houses on our beautiful land," they, in effect, tell themselves.

Since there is no other solution—they must either give up the estate entirely or rent small houses on it—they are without hope. They ask helplessly over and over, as if they had not heard the suggestion that they could rent houses, whether anyone can advise or help them.

Dr. Horney says that if their mentor were a good analyst, he would say, "Of course the situation is difficult. But what makes it hopeless is your own attitude toward it. If you consider changing your claims on life, there would be no need to feel hopeless."

Many times we are blind to our claims no matter who we are. You wouldn't expect this to be true of a psychiatrist, but it was. He told me the story himself. At one time, he lived on a five-acre estate in California; from his description it was something resembling the mansions in F. Scott Fitzgerald's *The Great Gatsby*, complete with swimming pool a half block away from the house, tennis courts, and a mile-long semicircular drive. "Things were going great for me," said my psychiatrist friend, "but then I took a huge risk in a land deal that I had no business being in and lost everything I had. It damned near did me in," he continued. "I threw myself around in a depression for months, hardly able to work, cursing my fate and my luck. What was even worse was the guilt I felt because here I was, a trained analyst, allowing myself to suffer so."

Finally, he moved to Florida, bought a four-bedroom, three-bath house that most of us would consider a beautiful home, and settled down to build another practice. "Boy, when I look back," he said, "I can't believe I suffered so, with all those grandiose claims

I warn other people about. I'll tell you this," he continued. "If I ever have to come down in life again, it will be much easier."

You Must Nurture Yourself

We all know that we should nurture ourselves, that we must befriend and like ourselves. I remember a sign in my dentist's office that says, "You only have to floss those teeth you wish to keep." It's the same with nurturing yourself. You only need do it if you wish to keep mentally healthy and effective. Otherwise, you can forget it.

Some people are lucky. They learn to be their own wise and kindly counselor early in life. When they have bad luck or poor judgment that causes them to make a mistake, they don't turn on themselves with self-contempt. As they go through life, they automatically give themselves messages of courage and hope. They are gentle with themselves, but disciplined.

Let me tell you about two men. One was an officer in the navy, the other in the air force; both are now retired. The retired navy officer is a friend of mine; the air force officer is the brother-in-law of a friend. Both, after twenty years of service, were passed over for promotion and had to leave the service. The potential for the devastation of a personality is the same with an officer in the services, rejected by his peers, as for a man or woman with a company who is let go.

My friend, the ex-navy officer, told me he started to go down the shute to self-contempt, and then, to use his words, "I decided to hell with it. It was the same bureaucratic machinery that screwed up at Pearl Harbor that made a mistake again with me. I knew I had to take care of and respect myself, for my sake and the sake of my family." My friend looked around, took a job as an instructor at a large eastern university and is now a tenured professor.

The air force officer, when he was passed over, decided to punish himself. The tyrant in his mind has condemned him as surely as a judge in a court but with none of the mercy that judge might show even a hardened criminal. This man floods his mind with messages of self-contempt, visits a psychiatrist twice a week, takes tranquilizers regularly and increasingly, and may never become a friend to himself again. He reviews endlessly one mistake he made that he is convinced caused him to be passed over. The mistake happened ten years ago!

If you could be this man's counselor, you would tell him something like this: "Yes, there's no doubt about it; you've had a terrible blow. For a man or woman to have a career snatched from them in mid-life is about as bad as it gets. Although there are, indeed, worse blows. You have a perfect right to be *sad*. You have suffered a loss. But come now, your talk of suicide, that your life is finished, that you're no good, isn't that a bit unrealistic, a little too harsh? Even if your peers are right that you're not the stuff that generals are made of, and they may be as wrong about you as they were about Billy Mitchell—but even if you're not the "right" stuff, must you then condemn yourself to a lifetime of suffering or give up life itself? Look at the rest of us who don't have the stuff to be anything grand; we still manage to like ourselves and enjoy life."

It isn't just passed-over officers in the service who must nurture themselves. We must all be a friend to ourselves, disciplining ourselves sometimes, being gentle with ourselves at others, always taking care of ourselves, giving ourselves good messages, remembering that mental health must always come first.

Sometimes you can get in touch with how hard you're being on yourself. You can actually *feel* the inner tyrant, unyielding, merciless. Even if your inner tyrant is not that active, you must become aware of what you do to yourself. As I said before, you can be certain you are tyrannizing yourself if you constantly feel pressure and often experience a feeling of effort, if you are usually hurried and behind in your work, if you suffer pervasive and unending guilt, if you're angry often, if you feel the need to please others or, conversely, feel they should please you, or if you feel that you must do everything with perfection and no mistakes. Whatever way you have chosen to rob yourself of freedom and happiness, you must ask what are the underlying statements and messages you are giving yourself that cause you to do this. "What am I telling myself?" must be your constant query.

You have no choice, really. If you are to use that three-pound miracle I spoke of, your brain, use more of those trillion cells and all their magic, you simply must give yourself messages of encouragement, hope, and health. This is the only way you can free this potential energy, the only way you can fully utilize this awesome instrument.

Become Aware of the Inner Tyrants

It's a difficult job becoming aware of the inner forces that rob us of peace of mind and happiness. But it's well worth the effort because the odds are that if you're tormenting yourself, you are just as hard on your friends and family; so any change benefits both you and them.

The inner tyrants are a "voice" in your head; you don't actually hear them in an auditory sense, but the message gets through. The inner tyrants wear pathways of automatic response in your mind; if you can't meet their unrealistic demands, you become depressed, anxious, full of self-contempt.

The inner tyrants demand that you make no mistakes, that you do everything perfectly, that you accomplish your goals in much less time than it takes most people, that you experience tension and effort in working toward your goals, that either you please others all the time, or they please you. Many times we'll be driven by only one or two of these inner demons, sometimes by all of them.

These inner tyrants often destroy our lives, but if we can become aware of them operating within us and know that this is brought on by ourselves, we can take charge of ourselves.

Tell yourself you are not going to succumb to the sickness of hurry. Effective people allow enough time to do the job and an extra margin for the inevitable interruptions and delays. They move forward at a steady pace and enjoy the work as much as they can. They remember that life is indeed a journey and not a destination and are not in a hurry to get every task behind them. They don't strive for perfection; they just try to do the job well. They don't feel constant pressure and effort but relax while they are working and get more done. They don't have the feeling of trying hard to do the job; they just do it.

Everything Considered, You're Doing Well

Tell yourself that everything considered, you're doing the very best you can. And tell yourself you must consider *everything*: your chances and opportunities, your genetic inheritance, the brains you were endowed with, the times you live in, the way the risk looked at the time you took it, the luck you've had. Telling yourself that fortune, the turn of the wheel, plays a role in your life doesn't mean you work and plan less, just that you don't tyrannize yourself.

And when you are doing Positive Programming, give yourself powerful messages of how well you have done so far. *Everything considered...everything considered*. Review and give yourself credit for the hardships, the suffering, the hard work, the effort, the planning, all the handicaps and heartaches. You, you must tell yourself, are in many ways a fine person, and you have tried to reach your goals. Why, of course you have made mistakes, sometimes big ones, but don't you really know that we all have? When you practice Creative Meditation, try to feel this fine person, locked up inside of you. Try to feel how terribly hard you have been on yourself at times and then let go; let up on yourself. In your Creative Meditation sessions give yourself positive suggestions to be a friend to yourself; repeat over and over that you must be kind to yourself. There is no value in tyrannizing yourself.

You Can Let Go

We often bombard ourselves with a storm of self-criticism, lashing ourselves with contempt, becoming irritable, discouraged, and unhappy. You must convince yourself that unbalanced, negative, critical inner messages poison your mind and undermine your health. It is impossible for you to bathe yourself in suggestions of defeat, failure, hopelessness, and melancholy and not live in that atmosphere and be crushed by it. *You don't have to do that to yourself*.

Tell yourself, "Let go!" Repeat it to yourself over and over until it becomes your mantra. Whether you are a harried housewife trying to keep your many duties balanced, a busy executive, a booked-solid professional, you do not need that *feeling* of effort and strain to work effectively; you will accomplish more and do it better without that feeling. Make your inner message this: "I've got work to do, so I'm going to relax." Remember William James' story about the man who loosened his hold and fell just six inches. Let go!

VIII

Creative Meditation for Worry, Fear, and Anxiety

> Some of your hurts you have cured.
> And the sharpest you still have survived,
> But what torments of grief you endured
> From evils that never arrived.
>
> *Emerson*

*O*ver the years much has been written about the habit of worry, because it is such a common malady and causes so much harm. Worry has been analyzed in essays, articles, poems, and entire books. Whenever my research turned up a new angle on the worrying habit and I broadcast it over my daily radio program, the write-ins for copies of the script were greater than for any other human problem I covered.

Yet for all the pages written about worry, there is one characteristic of the worry habit that is not mentioned, and that is its blocking function.

In learning theory it's well known that negative habits are a learned response. Even more important, it's known that a habit effectively blocks any other response.

Applied to worry, this means that if you have learned to respond to a problem with worry, then your worry habit will prevent you from responding any other way. And each passing day of your life you'll be reinforcing this destructive habit. (To divert here for just a moment, you can see that when applying this theory of blockage to another destructive habit, e.g. cynicism, that cynics are made and not born and that their cynicism, if deep enough, effectively blocks any other response.)

If you are the worrying type, you must do everything possible to extinguish this habit, and *the best way to do it is by replacing this learned habit with another habit*. (The same psychiatrist friend I mentioned earlier told me that excessive worry can actually change the chemistry in your brain and bring on a depression.)

I said the best way to stop the worry habit is to replace it with another habit, but how can you do that when, according to learning theory, a habit effectively blocks other responses? It takes conscious, deliberate reprogramming; it isn't easy, but you can do it in your Creative Meditation sessions with Positive Programming.

Here's how you do it. The second you start to worry, you form your "Light Touch" circle with thumb and forefinger of one hand. Just doing this will divert your mind for a second. As you make your "Light Touch" cue, remember to relax completely and repeat, over and over, your Positive Programming message. I'll go into more detail in just a moment, but first I want you to know that after you have done this a number of times, you will have programmed a new learned response in place of your worry response.

Now this routine may seem silly to some, but as the comedian said, "If you want silly, I'll give you silly." Silly is wasting your time and energy and creativity worrying about the future, silly is spending much of your time and energy being frightened about events that never happen, silly is becoming upset and irritable, silly is throwing yourself into a terrible and costly depression.

Think how much you would gain, how much more joyful your life would be if, instead of worrying, you had another response at your command, a phrase you repeated that gave you hope and comfort.

A daily schedule of at least two full Creative Meditation sessions combined with a number of instant meditation sessions will change the worry response you have perfected over the years and create new positive pathways. You will program yourself positively with hopeful, life-giving messages.

For a Full Creative Meditation Session

1. Form your "Light Touch" cue by placing your thumb and forefinger together, forming a circle, and completely relax.

2. Take one or several slow, deep breaths, whatever is comfortable for you.

3. Float for a minute or so. Think of nothing except making certain that your mind and body are completely relaxed. If your worry surfaces, gently push it aside and repeat your Positive Programming phrase, "I Choose Happiness," "Let Go and Let God," or another one you have selected. As you repeat your phrase, do it slowly in rhythm with your

breathing. Concentrate on your mantra and your breathing.

4. If your worry persists in surfacing, ask yourself or your "wise friend" what you are telling yourself to cause you to worry. Force yourself to define your worry in precise, definite words and tell yourself the whole truth about your worry.

There are three methods you can use to change your worry habit. You can use Positive Programming; you can use precise analysis, which often will help defuse the worry; and you can practice present-moment living to achieve a more relaxed and philosophical approach to life.

If you wish to analyze your worry, make certain you present to yourself a balanced and complete case. I remember meditating about an upcoming visit to a dentist. I tried to be as precise as possible in describing to myself past experiences. When I thought about it, I remembered the worst I had suffered was the sting of the lidocaine injection and, after that, considerable pressure but no pain. This helped me get over the dread of the visit. When I told my dentist about my "discovery," he said, "Nelson, you'd be surprised how many patients use the wrong word and thereby scare themselves. They think they're feeling pain when all it is is pressure."

5. In your Creative Meditation session repeat your Positive Programming message over and over and also repeat it to yourself many times during the day and evening and before you go to sleep. As I said earlier, your Positive Programming message will work for you if you calmly repeat your antiworry message over and over the instant you start to worry; you

will be replacing one habit with another. Believe me, it works! You will, in effect, be developing a new pathway in your mind while at the same time overriding the old response of worry.

Very often when we were young, we learned from observation that the conscientious way to handle a problem is to worry about it. Some people don't believe there is any other response. Gradually, over the years, we can develop worry "tapes" or "pathways" or responses that are so deeply rooted that we keep ourselves constantly uneasy.

I remember a friend in San Francisco who had a number of problems; he was not only getting older every day (there's a lot of that going around), but his small inheritance was running out. He couldn't find work, as most of his life he had lived in ease and luxury and really didn't know how to do much of anything other than be a Renaissance man, for which he found little demand.

I don't know whether he had ever heard of the word "mantra," but his wife told me he had an unusual way of soothing himself. He would close his eyes, gently rock back and forth, and repeat, almost under his breath, "It makes no difference." He found a strange peace in this phrase. I'm not recommending you use his phrase, although it evidently served him well. The last I heard from him, he had a good job with the city government and seemed to be living a good life.

While "It makes no difference" might not work for you, other mantras (Positive Programming messages) will. Here are a few to consider:

• *"It's not important."*
Obviously, this will not work for all situations,

such as a serious health problem or if you are out of work. But many of the problems we continuously worry about are far less serious.

- *"Everything works out for the best."*
  Of course, this sounds banal, but there is enough truth in it to help the worrier. I can remember event after event that appeared to be both crucial and to go the wrong way at the time but turned out for the best.

- *"It's only disagreeable, and I can handle that."*
  You and I certainly have the resources to handle that which is merely disagreeable. We can also bear discomfort. If something you are worried about will be only disagreeable and not a disaster, then telling yourself that you can handle it will take the worry away.

Here are a few religious antiworry mantras:

- *"Fear not! For I am with thee."*
- *"Be still and hear my voice."*
- *"If any man thirst let him come to me."*
- *"...hear me that your soul may live."*
- *"Let not your heart be troubled, neither let it be afraid."*
- *"I am with you always, even to the end of time."*
- *"The Lord is my shepherd; I shall not want."*

The instant you start to worry, use your worry as your cue to repeat your Positive Programming message over and over. If you change your worry habit, you will develop a different outlook and philosophy.

There are many excellent religious mantras. (I have not counted them myself but have read that in sacred Scripture there are 365 verses that have as their theme "fear not.")

A beautiful example from the Old Testament is given by Rabbi Mel Gottlieb:

> A few years ago, I was sitting in Jerusalem, in Novardock Yeshiva on the Shabbat between Rosh Hashanah and Yom Kippur, listening to a great musarnik, Rabbi Ben Tzion Brook. It darkened, evening came, and Rabbi Brook kept repeating one verse in sing song fashion from the Song of Songs 2:16:
>
> > My beloved is mine and I am my beloved's, who feeds among the lilies. My beloved is mine and I am my beloved's, who feeds among the lilies . . . God only wants a little bit of the lilies, a little bit of the heart of man. He doesn't want your automobiles. He doesn't want your coolness, your self-control, your closedness. He wants an open heart, a little bit of the lilies from each man.
>
> This singsong went on and on. He spoke to each man, to each heart, and after a while the bearded Jerusalemites sitting next to me began to beat their hearts. Tears began to flow. The fear, the control, the mistrust was shattered, and their full hearts were open.[1]

6. Ask yourself during your session, being as objective as possible, what is most likely to happen. When you hear hoofbeats, it's normal to picture a horse, but a fearful imagination will picture all sorts of weird animals. Remember that common things happen commonly.

It's difficult not to play "what if" in your mind: What if I get sick? What if the operation is not a success?

1. Mel Gottlieb, "The Musar Community," *Musar Anthology*, © 1972 by Hillel Goldberg, Harwich Lithograph (Hyde Park, Mass.)

What if I get fired? What if nobody likes me? What if I can't do it? But difficult or not, you must not play this mental game; no one can do it without scaring himself. Many people have told me that it's for this reason they get out of bed as soon as they wake up in the morning. If they lie there, half asleep, they start conjuring up all sorts of spooky ideas. A friend told me he got his contractor's license because during a stressful period in his life he kept waking up at 4:30 in the morning. He was thinking of changing jobs and would lie in bed worrying and endlessly reviewing his problem. "I did that for a few days, and it was too nerve-racking," he told me. "At that time in the morning every problem is magnified and seems scary. So I got in the habit of getting out of bed the minute I awoke, going into another room, and studying for my contractor's license. It's a great time to concentrate, and it sure beats worrying." In addition to his other talents, my friend is now a licensed contractor.

7. Ask, during your session, how you can get more facts. Facts are often friendly. Shakespeare said, "In the night, imagining some fear, how easy is a bush suppos'd a bear." With the illumination of facts, you can often see that the bear is a bush.

Recently, a friend of long-standing was faced with an operation. He was extremely upset, so I suggested, since he could not have been more worried, anyway, that he conduct a fact-finding mission, starting with the public library. He took the next afternoon off, read about his symptoms in several books, and after discussing the matter with his wife, decided it would be wise to seek a second opinion. The second doctor put him on a thirty-day prescription of an antibiotic that cleared up his symptoms. The doctor told my friend that as long as the antibiotic was effective, and he thought it would continue to be effective, he would advise against an operation, as often the scar tissue from that operation caused a great deal of trouble.

I'm not saying that facts are always friendly, but often they are; and it's always better to occupy yourself finding solutions to problems, trying to narrow the risks and work things out, than be caught in the reverberating circuit of worry, reviewing the problem over and over endlessly.

8. Give yourself the message "Start thinking" while you are in your Creative Meditation session and gently order the work to continue after you have ended your session. As I said earlier, many of us have formed a pathway when we worry that goes from the problem to worry and back to the problem again in a closed circuit. Often our response to the problem is to go into a "Don't think" mode and become confused and worried. Remember, when you tell yourself, "I'm confused," or, "I'm worried," that you are referring to an emotional state and not a mental one. You *feel* confused or worried; you don't think confused or worried.

One of the best questions to ask yourself in your sessions is, "What steps can I take?" Other questions might be: "Where can I get more information about my problem?" "How can I minimize my problem?" Don't press for answers. Stay as relaxed as you can. Gently ask, then step aside; you'll be amazed at the help you will receive. (For further ideas on problem solving, see chapter X.)

9. Ask if there are forces driving you that cause your worry. Telling yourself you always need *more* can very easily cause underlying anxiety

and fear. Tell yourself constantly that you need more money, power, position, or prestige, and there's a good chance you're heading for trouble. Of course, you can't blame someone for wanting a little hard currency if he has none. But there are instances of men and women with everything you could ask for still driving themselves on, worried every step of the way, until they finally overreach and lose everything from their health and peace of mind to their job, their power, and their money.

There's an old story about someone who held so much stock in one particular company that he told J. P. Morgan, I think it was, that he was so worried he couldn't sleep and asked J.P. what to do about it. "The answer is simple," said J.P., who had a knack of going to the heart of money matters. "Sell down until you can sleep."

Those who are driven to always grasp more, whether it's money, prestige, power, or glory, at the expense of their own and their family's peace of mind, need to "sell down" until they can relax, smell the roses, and broaden their outlook a little more. I often think of a friend of mine, a fiercely independent man who was in the Marine Corps most of his life. When he got out, he started a plant nursery from scratch by buying a used lawn mower and driving around in his car asking for jobs. Today he has one of the largest nursery and landscaping businesses in Florida. He's a real country boy in many respects; not the kind who says he is in order to deceive the unwary but the kind who is genuinely honest, works hard, puts on no airs, and plays no role. He gives everyone a good deal; he either charges less than he said he would or gives more than he promised. He's relaxed and at peace with himself.

Sometimes it pays to ask ourselves whether we are overreaching, driving ourselves and those we love too unreasonably, more interested in our goals than in our humanity, not realizing that our goals become our humanity. Ask yourself in your session if there are options, other ways of going about things that might give you greater satisfaction with less anxiety and worry.

10. Ask yourself if you're being fair.

Sometimes we become so determined to reach a goal that we, without being aware of it, become unfair in our dealings with others. This causes worry, uneasiness, and anxiety.

A man I know builds large luxury homes in a small city on the East Coast. He started the business about ten years ago and at that time was a relatively normal and happy individual. As he started selling his houses, he gradually discovered all kinds of ways to cut corners and use second-rate materials. In addition, he has a job with the city government. He is not even supposed to be building houses on the side, according to the terms of his contract with the city.

The last time we visited this couple, his wife told us their life had become a nightmare of lies, exaggerations, cover-ups, and denials. She said her husband seldom got a good night's sleep, was distracted and worried much of the time, and had started drinking excessively not only in the evening but during the day.

As a rule, when we're unfair, it's not as blatant and gross as the builder's actions, but unfairness, to any degree, will usually generate worry and anxiety. Use one of your Creative Meditation sessions to ask what you are telling yourself about your dealings with others and if this could be one of the sources of your worry.

11. Sometimes our fear is caused by an upcoming event that we view as threatening: a speech we must give, an interview we must go

through, an examination we must take, or a meeting we must conduct. Events such as these can cause us great discomfort because deep down we fear humiliation. This is a universal fear and, unfortunately, keeps many people from doing things they would enjoy and that would enhance their lives *even if once in a while they experienced humiliation.*

I'll never forget the remark of a musician who, when asked by an interviewer how he had the nerve to attempt writing a book when he had never written before, replied, "I'd like to try, man. Do you mind?" That must be what you tell yourself. "I'd like to try, man. Do you mind?" Sure, you'll want to avoid humiliation if you can, but if you experience flop sweat (Flop sweat is an inelegant term used by performers to describe a condition that occurs when you're in front of an audience, know that you're failing miserably, but it's too early in the performance to run and there is no place to hide. It's a terrifying experience, shattering at the time, but you live through it; almost all performers and speech makers experience it a few times in their lives.), eventually you'll look back on it and find it humorous. Here, again, you must tell yourself that even humiliation is only a feeling and that those who do anything must risk having to cope with it. One of the times I experienced the feeling, I was mistakenly booked, by a publisher, on a cooking show in Los Angeles to promote a book I had written that had absolutely nothing to do with cooking or anything remotely connected with cooking. I arrived late for the on-air interview. The M.C. of the program grabbed me, and we ran to the studio. The next half hour was pure torture and perhaps the worst radio program ever broadcast in the Los Angeles area, or maybe the funniest, but the host and I both lived through it, and now it has become amusing.

Tell yourself that the worst that can happen, and this may happen, is that you will not do as well as you would like but that you have the courage to handle that.

Visualize yourself giving the speech or performance, etc., in as much detail as possible. See yourself handling the situation with relaxed and calm efficiency, perhaps with a smile on your face. Remember how little children can remain so self-confident, even when they are in a room filled with strangers? That's because they assume that everyone will like them. That image of everyone being friendly to you should be in your mental picture. Keep that image of your being calm, friendly, and relaxed. Tell yourself that just before the event you will have several instant Creative Meditation sessions that will guarantee that you will be relaxed, calm, and eager to perform.

For an Instant Creative Meditation Session on Worry and Fear:

1. Use your "Light Touch" cue and become completely relaxed. Breathe slowly and comfortably.

2. Remember the point or points in the full session on worry that helped you the most.

3. Repeat your antiworry mantra over and over.

4. Remind yourself that fear is only a feeling and that our negative imagination always exaggerates.

5. Visualize your performance as you want it to be and remain calm and relaxed.

IX

Creative Meditation for Anger and Conflict

> He that is slow to anger is better than the mighty; and he that ruleth his spirit than he that taketh a city.
>
> *Proverbs 16:32*

> It is a question whether the great majority of people do not ruin their lives and mar their happiness by lack of self-control.
>
> *James Allen*

> In rage deaf as
> the sea, hasty
> as fire.
>
> *Shakespeare*

*W*hen we are quick to anger, it means that we have lost control of ourselves and are no longer in charge of what we do. Anger is a "racket" feeling in that it serves no purpose and does not move us along in life. (Anger at social injustice is often appropriate, but even here, if you are to be effective, it should be anger that is under control.) You can use Creative Meditation with Positive Programming to overcome your anger habit. Just giving yourself the "Light Touch" cue will divert you enough that you can remember your decision to take a more calm approach to life.

For a Full Creative Meditation Session

1. Form your "Light Touch" cue, take several comfortable breaths, and become completely relaxed.

2. Float for a few minutes. As you float, try to identify your feelings. If you are angry, ask if the anger is masking a deeper, underlying feeling such as hurt, rejection, inferiority, or threat. Don't press, and remember "it's only a feeling."

3. Continue to float until you feel calm and peaceful. The time this will take depends on the depth of your anger and the meaning it has for you. Start encouraging peaceful thoughts and pictures to enter your mind: a long-range goal you especially desire, an enjoyable evening, or perhaps, if applicable, a time when you and the person you've just had the argument with were getting along.

4. You may visit your haven, or you may continue floating. In either case, you may wish, eventually, to ask yourself one or more of the following questions. (Remember that you will be most effective by concentrating on only one aspect per session.)

   Why did I get angry?... the real reason.
   What role did I play in the anger drama?
   How can I take a lighter touch next time?
   Do I expect too much from others?
   Does anger help me get my way? Are there better ways?
   Can I learn to put off my anger? Can I substitute a Positive Programming message to extinguish my anger habit?

Can I play the adult role this time, heal the
breach, see the humor, perhaps be the
one to apologize?

I knew a man who was making over $100,000 a year
and was fired after an argument with his boss. I've
talked with him several times since he lost his job.
He's been out of work seven months now. Here is
what he and his wife and two children have had to do:
put the house up for sale, sell a small airplane he owned,
sell one luxury car, travel all over the country looking
for a job, reduce the salary he would now accept to
less than half what he was making (he'll be lucky if he
gets that), send out endless résumés, reduce all unnecessary expenditures to the minimum. In addition,
he worries constantly and has lost considerable weight.

When I last saw him, he told me there was a day or
two when he could have called his boss and smoothed
things over. "I don't know what the hell I was thinking," he said to me. "The district I was in charge of
was growing by leaps and bounds, and he wanted to
take away a very small part of it. It wasn't as if he
wanted me to change my religion or move to Africa.
I wouldn't even have taken a cut in pay."

I'm not saying that Creative Meditation would have
saved this man's job. I don't know that, of course. But
there should have been some way for him to get in
touch with himself, hear what he was telling himself,
be aware of the risks he was taking. During the day or
two when he could have made up with his boss, Creative Meditation might just possibly have helped him
to see the entire truth of the situation before it was too
late.

5. Always ask in your session, "What am I telling
   myself? Am I telling myself the whole truth?"

A woman had been having trouble with her teenage daughter. They were constantly fighting and tearing each other down. The woman told me that it came to her for the first time during a Creative Meditation session that she had been telling herself the wrong things about her daughter. "I had always gone on the basic, untested assumption that my daughter was not conscientious, sort of a goof-off. I think this general feeling about her started when she was in grade school and showed no motivation whatsoever. But now, here she was, graduated from high school with a good record, working almost full time, and paying a part of her tuition and expenses at a local university. Sure, her room was a mess, a disaster area, and the inside of her car was so loaded with school papers, newspapers, schoolbooks, and clothes, it looked like she was hauling trash, but I finally realized that none of this was important to me. So she's not neat; what difference does that make? I had been expecting perfection from a daughter who, everything considered, was doing very well working toward her goals."

6. Ask yourself, "How can I heal it?"

A number of years ago a sick stray cat came to our house, and several days later, despite the vet's efforts, it died during the night. One of my children, when he awakened in the morning and heard the news, was heartbroken and kept repeating over and over, "I didn't get to say good-bye." That strikes at the heart of the human condition. We so seldom, with those we love, get to say good-bye. Several years ago a woman who had worked very hard all her life to create a business and keep it going, watching every detail, alert to all risks, had a terrible argument with her son. The son stormed out of the house and that night was killed in an automobile accident. A dramatic, rare occurrence, yes, and yet we must always be aware that our being together is a prelude to good-bye.

There will always be anger, disagreements, and conflicts among those who care for each other. You can reduce the occasions by getting to the center of the problem, but since we are not saints, you will not eliminate them. Nevertheless, your orientation can always be, in your Creative Meditation session, "How can I heal this?" You can decide you will be the one who makes the approach; you can choose to be the peacemaker. I remember a woman who told us about a time in her married life when her husband had an affair with a woman in the office where he worked.

I was deeply hurt. But I finally figured out that life was questioning me and I could either give an average performance, throw our entire household up for grabs, or be understanding, realize that here was a middle-aged man desperately seeking reassurance, and then create a life for myself, my children, and him around the problem. It didn't last long, and he was a loving, attentive husband after that [He had died of a heart attack several years before she told us this story.] and the entire episode, looking back on it, is almost meaningless, so insignificant I can talk about it.

Remember that we always have the power to turn straw into gold. Visualize doing this in your sessions. Take what problem others may give you and use the alchemy of thought and love on it. I'm not saying you can handle every conflict this way, but the man I mentioned earlier, for example, could have learned to get along with his boss. We can learn to take the straw our loved ones sometimes give us and turn it into gold as much as we can. Do you need a spinning wheel to turn straw into gold? Rumpelstiltskin did, but we have the power within us and can weave this magic whenever we choose. It just takes an attitude, an orientation, and a willingness to exercise a little patience once in a while. You turn straw into gold by listening, first of all, and trying to think and feel as the other person. It calls for nonjudgmental listening and acceptance. And then, while you are listening, you carefully select what nuggets of truth and goodness you find, throw the bright light of understanding on them, perhaps magnify them a little, and lo and behold, you have created something valuable.

Of course, we have all seen the reverse alchemy take place when people take other's gold and turn it into straw: the friendly gesture ignored, the loving touch brushed aside, the brief cry for help in an argument passed over, the reaching out pushed back, the peace offering minimized or ridiculed. (See chapter V, "Straw into Gold," as a Positive Programming message.)

Ask yourself in your session, "How can *I* heal this? What can *I* do?"

7. Give yourself any of the following Positive Programming messages that are applicable to your situation:

- "I'm in charge." This is to remind you that you can control your anger and have decided not to let any rascal or situation that comes along upset your peace of mind.

- "I will be the peacemaker and cut this argument short." Always remember that this message and the action by you that follows not only makes you a more generous person but also puts you in control of the situation.

- "I will not make the issue important." Here

again, you are in control. You decide how important this issue is in your universe of living.

- "I will see the humor in the situation." When you shrink it just a little, take out all the overblown emotions, eliminate the unkind words that were not true estimates of character but merely weapons in battle, isn't it just a bit funny? Remember Scaramouch, "born with a gift of laughter and a sense that the world is mad."

- "I want to win." This sounds like a contradiction of what we've been talking about, and crass besides, but it isn't. It doesn't apply in many arguments or where important principles are involved, but it often does apply in a work situation. Men and women have quit jobs or been dismissed, changed their standards of living, given up much of what is important to them, moved their families from Key West to Alaska, and all because they wouldn't give in on relatively minor points. In this situation they would be well advised to give themselves the message in their Creative Meditation sessions that they want to win on those things that are important to them and their families, and that to do this they may have to be friendly and flexible on those issues that in the long run have no importance in their life at all.

For an Instant Creative Meditation Session

1. Form your "Light Touch" cue, take several comfortable breaths, and become completely relaxed.

2. Use whatever suggestions and ideas are applicable from the full session.

3. Remind yourself of your "win" motto if it is a work situation.

4. Tell yourself you will be at peace, you will be the healer in the situation, and you will be in control. Visualize yourself responding this way.

X

Creative Meditation for Decision Making and Problem Solving

> We shall succeed only so far as we continue that most distasteful of all activity, the intolerable labor of thought.
> *Learned Hand*

*M*an has been called a problem-solving animal, and it's true we must make decisions all the time. We're lucky that most of them are easy to make—what time to get up, what to eat for lunch, what to do in the evening. But there are hard ones, too; close ones to call: Should we refuse the promotion or take it and move to another city? Keep working or go back to school? As a woman, keep a hard-won position or stay home with a child? Have an operation or get a second opinion? Put a loved one in a nursing home, change jobs, get married, buy a bigger house?

In an interesting experiment on difficult differentiations, Pavlov, the famous physiologist, taught a dog that whenever he saw a circle, he would get food but would get nothing when he saw an oval. Then Pavlov made the ovals appear more and more like circles so that the dog couldn't differentiate between the two. After a number of days of this, the dog started running in circles, howling and displaying what could be labeled neurosis. The decisions were just too difficult to make. So when you feel uncomfortable or experience anguish when making a tough and close decision, don't feel as if you're weak or unusual. It can bring on neurosis and breakdown in human beings as well as in animals.

Creative Meditation can help you make decisions. First, it calms you down so that you're not filled with tension for fear of making the wrong decision. In addition, it allows your mind to freewheel, to tap your unconscious, and to come up with ideas and facts you may have forgotten. Creative Meditation is also a great retriever and synthesizer; your mental computer has a better chance of searching through the neurons in your brain for information you have stored but forgotten, combining the bits of information and, sometimes, giving you an answer you will think is amazing but which was there all the time waiting for you to become relaxed and aware enough to retrieve it.

It's not so improbable or hard to believe if you remember Jung's definition of the unconscious: that your unconscious is everything you know but of which you are not at the moment thinking, that it is everything perceived by your senses but not noted by your conscious mind, that it is everything that involuntarily and without paying attention to it you feel, think, want, and do. Think of that immense accumulation of knowledge you have stored away; think of how much better many of your decisions might be if you could utilize a small part of that knowledge; think how much better you might solve problems.

When faced with a tough decision or a problem, concentrate on it and list the pros and cons in your mind or on paper. Be certain you give yourself *permission to think* (see chapter V). George Bernard Shaw said that few people think more than two or three times each year and that he made an international reputation by thinking once or twice a week.

Avoid as much as you can the reverberating circuit type of activity that masquerades as thinking, where you go round and round, endlessly reviewing the same points. Actually *think*: compare, brainstorm, test, free-wheel, modify, research, gather data, examine.

Take as an example a woman who must decide whether to keep a hard-won position with an organization or stay home with a child. If she listens to the tapes in her head, most of which were put there by an earlier generation before there were many opportunities for women and before inflation, she could feel guilty if she didn't stay home. But you can't make a wise decision based on tapes.

The decision must be based on what is wise for this particular woman at this particular time. She must ask herself what is her "set," what is her own particular "style," and she must do a lot of freewheel brainstorming about the problem: maybe hire a loving grandmother type and pay her extra, ask the boss for a day off every two weeks for several years or ask if she can work at home one day a week, start the day an hour early and get home sooner, ask her husband to make a sacrifice or two, see if she can put in forty hours of work in four days' time, make Saturday afternoon "quality time" with the child, when she would actually enter his world and listen. (Many full-time parents don't give the children any quality time as opposed to "preoccupied time.") Come up with as many far-out solutions as possible to stimulate your thinking.

When you have exhausted all the forebrain thinking you can on the subject, give orders for the work to proceed underground. Walk away from the problem or go to sleep, but before you do, tell yourself your decision or solution will be wise. Edison, a genius at both finding and solving problems, would think about it for just so long and then lie down and take a nap. When he awakened, he would often have the solution.

We should use more than our forebrain for thinking, so after you have allowed time for your unconscious mind to work on the problem, have a Creative Meditation session to see if you can tap into the thinking that has been going on in your preconscious or unconscious.

For Your Full Creative Meditation Session

1. As you make your "Light Touch" cue, become completely relaxed and take several comfortable breaths.

2. Float for a minute or two, gently pushing aside distracting thoughts as they enter your mind.

3. You may wish to ask yourself or your "wise friend" any of the following questions that are applicable to your situation:

   • Am I making this an either/or decision when, in truth, there are other options or modifications in between?

   • Am I treating this as a life or death situation when it will not make that great a difference in my life? (There *are* decisions that have a momentous impact on our lives but not nearly as many as we think.)

• Am I treating this as a decision that will affect me for a lifetime when it need not be that permanent at all?

• If this is a business or investment decision, am I making time my ally? In other words, can I relax and let things work out, or am I counting on everything working out just right within a limited time period? In these situations it's best to remember that not only pride comes before a fall but greed, also. Sure, you want to do as well as you can, but quietly examine yourself to make certain you are not depending on luck or the optimism in the land to continue forever; it runs in cycles, as you know, and changes course with startling suddenness. If it must work out for you in a certain length of time, watch out!

• Ask yourself if there are any barely perceptible warning signals that you keep ignoring. That very often is your better judgment asking to be heard, and you should invite that material into your consciousness during your Creative Meditation session.

• Ask yourself what are the realistic expectations if you decide on a particular course of action.

• Finally, you might wish to ask the question that will end all your discomfort, "What should I do?" I would, however, tend to delay asking this question as long as circumstances allow. The longer you can delay, the better your decision is likely to be because of the work going on in another place in your mind. Be wary of any self-suggestions that are trying to please someone or that tell you you *should* do this or that. We all have obligations, but not as many as we might think, and our overriding obligation, provided we don't hurt anyone, is to ourselves.

Usually, one question per session is all you will be able to ask yourself effectively.

4. Tell yourself that when you finish your session, you will feel refreshed and relaxed. If you have not been given the answer that seems to be the perfect fit, then ask that the work continue in your unconscious after your session ends. The answer or answers may pop into your mind as you're walking around or in a dream or during your next session.

For an Instant Creative Meditation Session

1. As you make your "Light Touch" cue, become deeply relaxed and take several comfortable breaths.

2. Visualize yourself, comfortable and relaxed, thinking about your problem in a calm, judicious manner.

3. Ask yourself how you can move ahead just a little on the problem; can you inch ahead by defining it better, getting more facts, modifying it somehow?

4. Tell yourself that when you finish, you will be relaxed, calm, and creative. Program yourself positively; tell yourself that you will make a wise decision as soon as you need to.

After you have made your decision, if it's a major one in your life, you will want a Positive Programming message so you won't torment yourself by constantly reviewing whether you made the right decision. Your Positive Programming message will allow you to become wholehearted. In the example of the woman trying to decide between working and staying home with her child, her Positive Programming message might be "Everything considered, it's for the best." This, for her, can sum up the entire problem and all the thinking she did on it so that she doesn't have to review it endlessly in her mind. It's her cue to live with the decision and be happy with it. She should repeat her Positive Programming message many times during the day and in her Creative Meditation session. And to paraphrase a baseball player, "Don't look back; the inner tyrants may be gaining on you."

XI

Creative Meditation for Stress and Tension

> We must change ourselves from a race that admires jerk and snap for their own sakes, and looks down upon low voices and quiet ways as dull, to one that, on the contrary, has calm for its ideal, and for their own sakes loves harmony, dignity, and ease.[1]

A close friend of mine experienced chest pains for several days, and when he finally called his physician, was admitted to the intensive care unit in a hospital. He was monitored closely for several days, given tests, and then his doctor told him that it was 90 percent certain that the chest pains were not caused by his heart. The doctor thought his chest pains were caused by stress.

1. William James, *Talks to Teachers on Psychology: and to Students on Some of Life's Ideals* (New York: W. W. Norton & Co., Inc., 1958), p. 142.

My friend also thinks it's stress; he's been working over seventy hours a week for several years. The company he works for, a giant company among Fortune's top 500, has an excellent reputation for the management of its resources. And yet, in the case of my friend, they are allowing a human resource to be burned out. He told me:

> I guess my main trouble is my boss. In the twenty-two years I've been with the company, I've had tough ones, and I like to think that in some ways I'm a tough boss, but never one like this. He works seventy hours a week and has said, on more than one occasion, that if he can work that hard, all the executives under him can work that hard, also. He's not a bad guy, but there's no way to talk to him, to tell him you're hurting.

I discussed earlier the fact that the fight or flight syndrome built into the nervous system of primitive man no longer works for us. My friend doesn't have the choice of fighting or running. Here is unusual stress, over which he has little if any control, going on day after day for two years. His stress is not self-caused, nor does it exist only in his mind. It is existential; it is very real.

In addition to the long hours, there is other stress in his job. In this company, top management has instituted an evaluation program under which middle management is evaluated not only by those above them but by those below them. If you're in middle management, you know that no matter who you are talking to, they will one day be filling out an evaluation sheet on you. Try that on for tension.

I asked my friend if he felt threatened because of this over-and-under system of evaluation, and his *first* answer was that he didn't like being evaluated by those who worked for him, that he always felt as if he were walking on eggs when he told them what to do; later, he said he didn't mind the constant evaluation; finally, he said, "I'm my own worst critic." You can hear the gears strip as this good man goes from trying to meet his own needs in the company to being the loyal company executive that he is. His first answer is he doesn't like it, his second is it's okay, and the third answer, about being his own worst critic, doesn't bear directly on his problem.

My friend's seventy-hour workweek, with constant evaluation taking place, will not go away simply by meditating on it, but meditation would help him and his family. It helps everyone experiencing stress and tension, whether self-caused or brought on by outside forces.

My friend could use it to straighten out what he's telling himself. "I'm my own worst critic" is a vague statement, and Creative Meditation could bring him closer to the whole truth. Of course he criticizes his performance, perhaps unnecessarily, but who wouldn't if they were always aware that those they work with will be filling out evaluation sheets. (If I sound as if I'm against evaluation sheets, I'm not. But any evaluation program must be handled with the greatest sensitivity and not be done too frequently. Many safeguards must be built into it, and those who read them must be constantly aware that man is often a poor judge and a biased one of his fellow man, and there must be periods when there is a letup.)

I haven't talked at length and in specific detail with my friend about his problem, so I don't know everything involved in his particular situation, but during his Creative Meditation sessions he could explore some of the following areas:

- What is it exactly that he fears? The Young Turks under him who evaluate him? That he's an older man in a company increasingly dominated by those younger than he is? That although he has twenty-two years' experience with his organization, he does not have the education or the high grade point average that many of those under him achieved?

- Does he fear possible humiliation if he can't keep up?

- Does he fear that the organization, by requiring that he put aside his home life, is robbing him of his values?

- Does he fear that once again the company will uproot him and his family, with all the family pain that entails, and send him to yet another strange city to live?

- Does he fear that he will lose his long and carefully cultivated self-control and tell his boss off?

The above questions and those like it would help my friend define his problem precisely so he can start telling himself the truth about it and then set about finding specific answers to specific problems. In addition, if he would have at least one session daily, he would be able to give himself minutes of peace and relaxation, and he could search for creative ways to help himself. Only the person involved in a problem can come up with the exact answer for himself, but here again there are many areas to explore: talking the problem over more with his family to relieve the stress, jogging or other forms of exercise, asking for a transfer to a different boss in the same city, taking early retirement, visiting a nearby university and asking the heads of the departments of management, psychology, or human resources if there are any professors available to consult with, attending stress seminars, seeking therapy, or maybe deciding to stick it out but work on changing his attitude.

And if he meditates about it, he'll come up with other answers, too. Of course a solution is difficult, but not nearly as difficult as doing nothing and perhaps shortening your life.

I have also talked with my friend's wife about their problem. She is a fine, compassionate woman who is a full-time homemaker, and she and her husband are very close. That he is under stress has placed her under stress, also. She can help him greatly if she also has Creative Meditation sessions, gets in touch with her innermost center, asks how she can keep herself, her children, and her home peaceful so that he has a place where he can relax and find rest.

Finally, they both need to formulate an antistress mantra that will help them channel a new pathway in their mind. One of the Positive Programming messages in chapter V of this book might help them, or perhaps they can formulate one of their own. Oh, come now, you might say, how can an antistress mantra help him when he's working a seventy-hour week for a boss he doesn't like?

The problem could, just could, be his attitude, and if he can't change his boss, and nothing else works, he may have to change his attitude. It's often not that you're working hard and long hours that causes stress, but that you're working long hours at something you've told yourself you don't like.

Since both husband and wife asked my advice, I talked with them about the benefits of Creative Meditation and told them that while it would not make their problem disappear, it might give them an answer concerning it or change their attitude about it. At the very least, it would give them relaxation and keep the problem from overwhelming them.

Now that they know about Creative Meditation, will they do it on a regular basis? Well, only time will tell. Although I don't think my friends are in that category, there are thousands who will not try anything to help themselves: seat belts; vitamins; exercise; adequate sleep; not smoking, overeating, or overdrinking; or, for that matter, even flossing their teeth!

Self-Induced Stress

The stress my friend working the seventy-hour week experiences is caused primarily by forces outside himself. Much of our stress, however, is caused by ourselves; it's self-inflicted.

Another close friend kept himself under stress for years. He had an unusual habit of calling people long distance and then being so distracted and pressured he'd tell them he didn't have time to talk. He called me a number of times: I'd pick up the phone, say "hello," and he would say, "Nelson, I don't have time to talk right now. I'll call you later." When he was in town we often went out to dinner, and he kept himself aquiver making phone calls, writing himself notes, looking at his watch.

My friend wasn't stupid; he was above average in intelligence and a top executive with a major company. But from morning till night he was ridden by the clock. He told me he had not had a vacation with his family for over ten years; he didn't think he could be away from his job that long. It saddens me to say that he's away from his job permanently now; he died last year as the result of a heart attack. Was the heart attack induced by his self-inflicted stress? Of course that's difficult to answer, but his physician thinks it was at the very least a contributory factor.

Conditional Living

Many of us live under constant stress because we lead *conditional* lives. This means we only feel good about ourselves under very strict conditions. We feel good about ourselves *only if*:

- We make a superhuman effort and then try even harder.
- We work all the time.
- We do things in less time than others or less time than *anybody* could do it.
- We keep the numbers climbing (income, size of house, net worth, cost of car, etc.).
- We keep others in the shade.
- We make absolutely no mistakes.

You're probably wondering if it isn't natural to work hard to achieve a distant goal. The answer is: Yes, of course it is. I don't know any other way. And the way to do this and keep at it steadily, to open your mind to great creativity, and to tolerate setbacks along the way and yet keep going is to take very good care of yourself and get rid of the inner tormentors who cause you to become discouraged, depressed, hopeless, and full of self-contempt. The calm and serene person is at peace with himself and others; he can work at a steady pace, enjoy what he is doing, expect a few mistakes and shrug them off, and allow himself enough time for the inevitable delays and interruptions.

If you feel pressured by time, constantly struggling to achieve more and more in less and less time, do yourself a favor and read *Type A Behavior and Your Heart* by Meyer Friedman and Ray H. Rosenman. It just might lengthen your life.

And whether your stress is caused by forces over which you have little or no control or by your own inner tormentors, give yourself the gift of at least three minutes a day in Creative Meditation. This is little enough time to spend in enriching your mind and spirit.

For Your Full Creative Meditation Session

1. Form your "Light Touch" circle by just barely touching your thumb and forefinger. Let this remind you to become completely relaxed, take life with more of a light touch, and to *slow down*. Use this as a cue to remind you to get off hurry-up time.

2. Take several slow, comfortably deep breaths to help you relax.

3. Double-check to make certain you have relaxed your muscles, especially your neck, shoulder, and facial muscles.

4. Ask what you are telling yourself to cause your stress:

   • Am I striving for a level of perfection that is neither achievable nor necessary? Rather than being perfect, can I achieve more by just doing well?

- Isn't my inner demand for perfection merely a way I tyrannize myself and keep myself from enjoying my accomplishments?

- Do I avoid activities I would enjoy because I can't do them perfectly?

- Am I on hurry-up time? Am I more concerned with the clock and the passing of time than I am with the task at hand? Since I often feel the pressure of time, isn't this just another way I tyrannize myself, making certain I don't enjoy the task or the passing moment? (Fully functioning people don't do this to themselves.)

- Do I associate work and accomplishment with tension, effort, and the feeling of trying hard? Can't I really tap more of my creativity if I let go? Isn't it true, as William James said, that you can get much more done if you relax? Why have I made time my enemy? Why can't I relax?

5. Ask yourself how many of your present accomplishments you owe to impatience. Granted, to catch a plane you must be at the airport on time, but do you really need that feeling of rushing as a dominant force in your life? You may say it's essential, but there are others who accomplish as much as you, or more, who would say you are driven, not completely in charge of yourself. There is an interesting story told about the great physiologist Ivan Pavlov, whose experiment on difficult differentiations I described on page 134. He is best remembered for his discovery that dogs would salivate when he substituted an artificial stimulus (a bell) for a natural stimulus (food). It was Pavlov who labeled this now well-known reaction a conditioned reflex. The

story is that as he was dying, his students crowded around his bedside and asked him the secret to a successful life. He told them the secret was contained in just two words: "passion and gradualness."

6. Visualize yourself slowing down and accomplishing just as much. Ask yourself or your "wise friend" how you can do this. Maybe you're lucky and are in a position to have others help you a little more, to let go of a few things. Or maybe you can reduce the time you spend on unimportant things. Perhaps you keep a check on everything and everybody in your life and pay too much attention to details that are really unimportant.

7. Ask your "wise friend" how you can reduce your stress and tension. Trust your "wise friend" more than your inner tyrant.

8. Give yourself a powerful suggestion that when your session ends, you will feel relaxed and comfortable. Tell yourself that during your day you will remember the feeling you are now experiencing and that this will help you with your stress and tension. Become conscious of good body feelings so that you can recreate them at will.

9. Tell yourself that at the count of four you will feel relaxed, refreshed, and in complete charge of yourself, your work, and the pace of your day.

For an Instant Creative Meditation Session

1. Form your "Light Touch" cue, breathe slowly and comfortably, and become completely relaxed.

2. Ask what messages you are giving yourself to cause your stress and tension. You might wish to examine: Are you fighting the clock? Do you expect yourself to do things in a hurry and do them perfectly?

3. If the cause of the stress is obvious and there is nothing you can do to change it, ask yourself how you can handle it more effectively.

4. Repeat to yourself any of the following mantras that are applicable and that you find helpful:

> "I'm going to relax and get more done."
> "It's only disagreeable, and I can handle that."
> "Effective people work at a relaxed pace and do one thing at a time."
> "I'm in charge, not some inner tyrant driving me on."

5. Visualize yourself as calm and relaxed.

6. Tell yourself you will feel relaxed and refreshed, be more in control, and move at a more effective pace.

XII

Creative Meditation When You Feel Hurt, Unappreciated, or the Victim of Injustice

Any hardship becomes ten times harder if we consider it unfair.

Karen Horney

The habit of being happy enables one to be freed, or largely freed, from the domination of outward events.

Robert Louis Stevenson

I realize I'm presenting only one side of the story, but this is the way the young man told it to me. He had married several years earlier, and his wife, who had been orphaned as a child, was not only in love with the young man but was also pleased to become part of his family. "Both of us," he said, "wanted very much to get along with my mother, but she made it impossible." The young man also said:

She was constantly hurt. No matter how many times we called her, she said it wasn't enough. My wife wrote her at least twice a week, and that

151

wasn't enough. We told her she had an open invitation to visit us as often and for as long as she pleased, but she refused to make the trip. There was never one time I talked to her on the phone that she didn't complain about something, implying I was not treating her right. It doesn't sound like much when you tell it, but it kept my wife and me constantly upset.

Some people would rather feel hurt than happy. Perhaps this mother was such a person. Almost all of us get our feelings hurt from time to time and think we're the victim of injustice, but it's best to keep tabs on ourselves to make sure it doesn't become a habit.

Some people, when they are the victim of real or imagined injustice, receive such a strange satisfaction that they will go out of their way to collect a grievance or a hurt. One young woman I know, because of a mix-up in transferring credits, was one course shy of receiving her high school degree. Believe it or not, she allowed herself to become so overwhelmed by the injustice of it that she never went back to take the course and receive her degree. Years later, she recounts how severely this incident hurt her. Granted, it was an injustice, but to spend the rest of her life feeling hurt doesn't make sense.

In *The Great Divorce*, which has to do with heaven and hell, not with human marriage, C. S. Lewis speaks about a woman who feels so aggrieved that she has turned from a grumbler into a grumble with no trace of the real woman left. Lewis says, "... it begins with a grumbling mood, and yourself still distinct from it: perhaps criticising it ... Ye can repent and come out of it again. But there may come a day when you can do that no longer. Then there will be no *you* left to criticise the mood, nor even to enjoy it, but just the grumble itself going on forever like a machine."[1]

In some families the husband or the wife may tell themselves they are mistreated and enjoy the role of victim. Parents tell themselves their children are unfair and nurture the feeling of hurt; children think their parents do not treat them right and carry with them all the burdensome baggage of the perpetual victim. There are even people who claim they have a right to feel hurt because they were abused in their childhood and others who proudly display their hurt feelings because of a humiliation suffered by their grandparents.

Then there are others who do not feel victimized by any particular person but by life, or fate itself. Their major message to themselves, which they repeat over and over, is "It's unfair. It's unfair."

There is no doubt that life is unfair. There is no doubt that people treat people unfairly. Every day you see examples of life handing out large helpings of good and bad luck indiscriminately. But you can increase your happiness and effectiveness so very much if you train yourself to view people and events not as fair or unfair but just the way they are. Don't tell yourself something is unfair; tell yourself that's merely the way it *is*. (See, in chapter V, the Positive Programming message "It is not 'unfair'; it just 'is.'") Give up your claims that if life or people do not treat you a certain way, it's unfair. These claims will bring you nothing but bitterness and unhappiness. In her book *Neurosis and Human Growth*, the brilliant psychiatrist Dr. Karen Horney says:

The effects which pervasive claims have on a personality and his life are manifold. They may

1. C. S. Lewis, *The Great Divorce* (New York: The Macmillan Company, 1946), p. 72.

create in him a diffuse sense of frustration and a discontent so encompassing that it could loosely be called a character trait. There are other factors contributing to such chronic discontent. But among the sources generating it, pervasive claims are outstanding. The discontent shows in the tendency in any life situation to focus on what is lacking, or on what is hard, and thus to become dissatisfied with the whole situation. For instance, a man is engaged in a most satisfactory work and has a family life which is largely constructive, but he has not enough time to play the piano, which means much to him; or perhaps one of his daughters has not turned out well; and these factors loom so large in his mind that he cannot appreciate the good he has. Or consider a person whose otherwise pleasant day can be spoiled by the failure of some ordered merchandise to arrive on time—or one who experiences in a beautiful excursion or trip only the inconvenience. These attitudes are so common that almost everyone must have encountered them. Persons having them sometimes wonder why they always look on the dark side of things. Or they dismiss the whole matter by calling themselves "pessimistic." This, aside from being no explanation at all, puts on a pseudophilosophical basis an entirely personal incapacity to tolerate adversities.

Through this attitude people make life harder for themselves in many ways. *Any hardship becomes ten times harder if we consider it unfair.* (Italics mine.)[2]

Remember, you can make life ten times *easier* for yourself if you give up the claim that people and events

2. Karen Horney, *Neurosis and Human Growth* (New York: W. W. Norton & Co., Inc., 1950), pp. 57, 58.

treat you fairly. You will still have the hardship, slight, rejection, or humiliation to deal with, but you will not need to suffer the unproductive feeling of being victimized.

For Your Full Creative Meditation Session

1. Form your "Light Touch" cue, take several slow, comfortable breaths, and become completely relaxed.

2. Float for a minute or two and feel your hurt; identify it as "only a feeling."

3. Ask yourself or your "wise friend" what you tell yourself to cause this feeling. Are your expectations of others unreasonable? Do you expect others to drop everything to take care of a need of yours? Do you realize that other human beings have a difficult time taking care of their needs, surviving, making a living, and feeling good about themselves and that often, even though they may love and respect you, they just don't have the time or energy to meet your demands?

4. You might wish to ask yourself if you play the role of victim often. Are you often angry or hurt because of some slight? There should be no humiliation in admitting this. The victim role is terribly beguiling, and there are many of us walking around feeling as if we have been hurt by fate, loved ones, or friends. Ask yourself if there are not better feelings to have.

5. Ask what the victim role does for your relations with others. Do they love you more for

it? Do they want to help you more? Does it get you what you really want or need? What role would serve your needs better? If you think it's true that you are giving much more than you are receiving and you feel hurt because of this, then might it not be wise to stop giving as much and feeling hurt less?

6. Tell yourself that feeling hurt and unappreciated is unproductive and you intend to stop. Tell yourself your philosophy is that life or people are neither fair nor unfair; they just are the way they are. Remind yourself that you intend to go for the good feelings, that you will be in charge, that whatever comes along you will handle and not play the role of victim.

7. Visualize yourself as a contented person, happy and in control of your feelings, "freed from the domination of outward events."

8. Repeat your Positive Programming message "It is not 'unfair'; it just 'is.'"

For an Instant Creative Meditation Session

1. Form your "Light Touch" cue and completely relax. Breathe deeply and comfortably.

2. Repeat your Positive Programming message:
   "I refuse to play the role of victim."
   "I choose happiness."
   "It's not 'unfair'; it just 'is.'"

3. Tell yourself you will feel good and in control of your feelings.

4. Visualize yourself this way.

XIII

Creative Meditation When You Are Unhappy

> ...he looked not for the damning but for the saving element in what he saw: a mental attitude that surely, if unexpectedly, provides the only road to truth. This optimism had much more than a temperamental basis...it was a conviction rooted deep in thought.[1]

> Peak experiences do not last, and cannot last. Intense happiness is episodic, not continuous.
>
> *Abraham H. Maslow*

We know from our own experience that intense happiness is not continuous. But intense *unhappiness* can last a long time and is one of the greatest torments a human being can experience. If you, a loved one, or a friend are experiencing intense unhappiness, then, as I have said before, you need professional help, and it's best you seek it right away. Don't delay. You may not believe it, but many professionals in the field of mental health can do wonders for you.

A friend, who works for a large company, threw

1. Pierre Teilhard de Chardin, *Letters from a Traveller* (New York: Harper and Row, 1962), p. 17 of the Introduction by Pierre Leroy.

himself around for three months in the throes of a moderately severe depression. He was extremely unhappy with his career and almost resigned from his company, where he had worked for twenty years. Finally, after much suffering, he sought the help of a psychiatrist, who took him off the tranquilizers he was taking and prescribed an antidepressant drug in a carefully controlled dosage. My friend *snapped out* of his depression in two weeks' time. I put "snapped out" in italics because that's exactly what happened, as my friend described it. He said:

> Nelson, it seemed like a miracle, and it happened just the way the doctor said it would. For months I had been depressed, not caring if I lived or not, in fact hoping that I wouldn't, and then one morning, after taking the medicine for two weeks, I awoke, and I knew immediately that I was thinking normally, the exaggerated fears were gone, the depression was lifted. The first thing I did was rush to the kitchen and exclaim to my wife, "It's happened. The medicine has worked; the depression is lifted. I'm back."

If you're depressed, you'll very likely think that no one can help you, that it's just the circumstances you're in that make you unhappy, and you'll doubt that anyone can possibly change your circumstances. I talked to a friend who is a psychiatrist and asked his opinion on this point. He said just about what you'd expect: that in a depression there are often strings that are connected to the person's real-life situation but that the depressed person magnifies his problems until they are overwhelming and all out of proportion.

So if your unhappiness is deep or your fears are many or you worry all the time, please seek professional help. Don't continue to suffer alone.

At any one time most of us are not intensely unhappy but have periods when we are negative about life, periods when we're bored or just not getting much enjoyment from our life. We're not intensely unhappy, just sort of down on life. What can we do?

The first characteristic of happiness that we all need to remember is that it is, indeed, episodic. It comes and goes. No one is happy all the time; in fact, it wasn't until just recently in the history of man that people even expected to be happy most of the time. It's a new development that came about because most of us have been able to satisfy our basic needs. This allows us the luxury, then, of asking ourselves if we are happy. A hungry person doesn't spend time asking if he's happy; he's much too busy looking for food.

Abraham Maslow, who formulated the hierarchy-of-needs theory, with the self-actualizing person being the one who has satisfied all his lower needs and is now in the process of becoming all he can become, said this:

Another addition to the description of self-actualizing people emerged from my study of "grumbles" [Grumbles are people who are never satisfied. Surprisingly, both C. S. Lewis and Abraham Maslow wrote about "grumblers." Both writers were very precise in their use of language, and "grumble" was exactly the word they wanted.] and the widespread tendency to undervalue one's already achieved need-gratifications, or even to devalue them and throw them away. Self-actualizing persons are relatively exempted from this profound source of human unhappiness. In a word, they are capable of "gratitude." The blessedness of their blessings remains conscious.

Miracles remain miracles even though occurring again and again. The awareness of undeserved good luck, of gratuitous grace, guarantees for them that life remains precious and never grows stale.[2]

If your unhappiness is not severe and continuous, then Creative Meditation can help you greatly, and here's how to go about it.

For Your Full Creative Meditation Session

1. Form your "Light Touch" cue, breathe slowly and comfortably and become completely relaxed.

2. Ask if you are causing your unhappiness and, if so, why you are doing it and how you are doing it. Very often the first step in relieving your unhappiness is for you to feel that it is something that you are doing to yourself. Sometimes it is very difficult for us to realize that we are keeping ourselves down. Unhappiness is not always self-administered, but it is more often than the average person would suspect. Lincoln recognized this when he said, "Most people are about as happy as they make up their mind to be."

3. Ask what you are telling yourself to cause your unhappiness. You might wish to ask your "wise friend" why, if it isn't apparent to you, you are unhappy and what you can do to become happy again.

2. Abraham Maslow, *Motivation and Personality*, 2nd ed. (New York: Harper and Row), p. xxi.

4. Ask yourself: "Is this really what I want to do to myself?" Even if you have suffered a loss or a disappointment, do you really want to add to it by beating down on yourself with no mercy?

5. Ask yourself if your unhappiness is caused by someone hurting your feelings. Do you feel as if no one loves or cares for you? We all need love, but if we can't satisfy this need, and most of us go through periods in our lives when we can't, then do you really think this calls for you to turn on yourself and make yourself unhappy? Wouldn't a more appropriate response be for you to take even better care of yourself, give yourself even more encouragement than you usually do, treat yourself more kindly? Won't you receive more love if you have a calm center of self-esteem where you take care of yourself and don't need to demand it of others? Granted, we all seem to want love desperately, but must you turn on yourself if you don't get it?

6. Ask whether you aren't, perhaps, taking your unhappiness a little too seriously. Naturally, we all want to be as happy as we can. It's a good feeling, but it's only a feeling. Do you tell yourself the rest of us are happy all the time, with no problems, troubles, or fears? Joshua Liebman said:

> The basic tragedy of humanity is that while each individual can understand only himself directly, he can know what goes on in other human lives only by inference. We torment ourselves by attributing perfection, joy, happiness to others. They make the same mistake about us. Most human beings do not carry their

hearts on their sleeves; all live a life partially of pretense and appearance. Every human being has limits, imperfections, frailties. Happiness is unobtainable until one makes his peace with this emancipating truth.[3]

Can you believe that? Can you believe that the rest of us have much the same accumulation of hopes and fears as you have? We hide behind a facade of smiles and lightheartedness, but we are trying just as you are to get from here to there in life. Perhaps the main difference is that some of us constantly fan the flame of hope. You might remember that you must have hope; it's one of the major virtues, and you have no chance for happiness without it.

7. During your session remember moments in your past and identify with them. That was also you; you were happy then, and things worked out for you. They will again. Know that, although you may be unhappy at the moment, you are not an unhappy person.

8. Give yourself a powerful suggestion that when you end your session, you will feel at peace with yourself, that you will choose happiness. It's sometimes very helpful if you, while in your session, promise to give your "inner child" a treat when you finish—a shopping trip, lunch with a friend, a set of tennis, a movie, a call home, etc. Take an active role in cheering yourself up.

9. Always end your session by repeating several times your Positive Programming message. Tell

3. Joshua Loth Liebman, *Hope for Man* (New York: Simon and Schuster, 1966), p. 147.

yourself you will repeat this message many times during the day.

For an Instant Creative Meditation Session

1. Form your "Light Touch" cue, breathe slowly and comfortably, and become completely relaxed.

2. Remind yourself that *you* are making yourself unhappy and that you don't have to do that to yourself. Ask what you are telling yourself to make you suffer.

3. Prior to your instant sessions you will have read chapter V, "The Power of Positive Programming," and selected one of the messages. Repeat this message several times and tell yourself you will continue repeating it during the day.

XIV

Creative Meditation and All Those Guilt Feelings

Every guilty person
is his own hangman.
Seneca

That mind and soul, according well, may make one music.
Tennyson

M*any people walk around with a pervasive feeling* of guilt. They cause themselves to suffer and miss the joy in life. They, in effect, tell themselves they don't deserve any better. They may feel guilty for any number of reasons: they are rich, poor, successful, blessed with luck, divorced, out of a job, oversexed, undersexed, not good enough to their parents, didn't raise their children right, messed up on the job, were not kind enough to their late Aunt Minnie, do not have enough friends, waste their time—there is no end to what we human beings may feel guilty about.

164

Often we strive for an impossible perfection and feel guilty when we can't attain it. A man or woman works long hours and feels guilty for quitting from exhaustion; a woman raises her children without a husband and feels guilty because the bum ran out on them; a child knocks himself out but can't please his parent and feels guilty. We set up unrealistic, idealized images of how life should be and then feel guilty when we fall short.

And although guilt is an excellent do-it-yourself activity, there are any number of people who will invite you to feel guilty. I say "invite" because that is really all it is—an invitation. It's up to you whether to accept or decline the invitation.

I think it was Abraham Maslow who said that much of the guilt we feel is "silly guilt." It serves no positive function. Maslow thought that healthy people did feel guilt, but only about such things as their own improvable shortcomings, such as laziness, unkindness, envy, prejudice, or irritability.

We all carry at least a little baggage of silly guilt. We stew about things in the past that can never be changed; we condemn ourselves over real or imagined transgressions that are over and done with; we agonize over mistakes that cannot be corrected.

Silly guilt is not constructive, but it does serve hidden purposes. You can feel guilty for a ten-hour shift, and it does nothing to change the past, but it does serve psychological processes for the person feeling guilt. It's a great way, for example, to avoid making amends or to keep from changing. If you feel so very bad about what you have done, then you certainly couldn't be expected, on top of how bad you feel, to make amends or change your behavior. They couldn't expect all your self-inflicted punishment and that, too! It also serves to mask present-moment living and make it unimportant, because your energy is concentrated on thinking about past errors; your main goal is centered on struggling with the past rather than living in the present.

And since many human beings, for strange and usually unknown reasons, have a need to suffer at least once in a while, guilt is an excellent way to do it. The inner tyrant can accuse you of all sorts of mischief, misbehavior, and errors and thus not only keep you from enjoying the present moment but so cloud your mind that you don't even consider how you might change your ways.

In your Creative Meditation session visualize silly, unproductive, and overactive guilt as a tape in your head softly playing your "shoulds": "You should have done this; you shouldn't have done that." Should, should, should, over and over, drowning out with constant criticism the growth-producing message "All things considered, you're doing a fine job."

Silly guilt is not always easy to extinguish. It's a habit and often a deeply ingrained one. Remember, I said that a habit blocks all other responses. In other words, you can't extinguish your habit of feeling guilty merely by an act of the will. When the guilt feeling pops into your mind, it blocks other responses. You can, however, use your guilt as a cue to cut in with your Positive Programming message "I Choose Happiness," or, "Don't Make It Important." Do this often enough and long enough and you will extinguish your guilt habit.

A number of writers state you should do away with all guilt feelings, that they are nonproductive. I don't agree with this. First of all, most of us have a moral code, and we feel guilty when we break it. But even here it pays to make amends, do what we can to atone, and then firmly put it behind us. It's unproductive to recreate the misdeed in our mind over and over and then feel guilt because of it. You're not helping anyone by merely feeling bad.

Joy and happiness are the emotions to go for in life, not guilt. Creative Meditation can help overcome guilt feelings that are useless. Here's how to go about it.

For Your Full Creative Meditation Session

1. Become fully relaxed using your "Light Touch" cue. Take several comfortable breaths.

2. Float for a minute or two and examine your guilty feeling. Try to feel how *you* are causing yourself to suffer.

3. Ask what you are telling yourself, specifically, to make you feel guilty.

4. You might wish to visualize yourself as a child and ask the child, specifically, what he is guilty of. Let the child explain himself fully. Then visualize yourself as a very wise adult explaining to the child the logic of the situation, that it is a great waste to continue punishing himself. If it's applicable, give the child something appropriate to do to atone and then tell the child he is forgiven, that it's past and over with. (It's surprising how effective this is.)

5. If you don't wish to visualize yourself as a child, then as an adult tell your guilt to your "wise friend." Ask what is the intelligent, loving thing to do about it.

6. Tell yourself that you are not going to be the cause of your own undoing; you are neither

that unintelligent nor that self-destructive. Give yourself an antiguilt mantra. Say to yourself, "Surfeit! Enough! Self-inflicted suffering is silly!"

7. Tell yourself how destructive it is to live looking backwards, focused on the past. Give yourself the message that you will feel very good about yourself. You will accept yourself *unconditionally*, with all your human imperfections, and will enjoy your hours on this earth.

8. Visualize yourself happy and relaxed. Tell yourself, "I intend to live facing forward."

For Your Instant Creative Meditation Session

1. Form your "Light Touch" cue and become deeply relaxed.

2. Repeat your antiguilt mantra over and over: "You are forgiven. You are forgiven," or, "God accepts me and I accept myself." Let go. Feel *you* letting yourself up.

3. Tell yourself when you finish you will no longer feel that inner weight bearing you down. You will feel free. You will experience joy.

XV

Three Minutes a Day

> Man does not simply exist, but always decides what his existence will be.
>
> *Viktor Frankl*

Ten to twenty minutes a day would be the ideal time to spend in your Creative Meditation sessions, but there are many who will not set aside ten to twenty minutes each day. Some people don't have that much spare time, or at least think they don't. So let's be practical.

If, in your mind, you are quite certain you will not stick to the practice of ten to twenty minutes of Creative Meditation, then promise yourself at least three minutes a day. This will keep you in the habit and give you daily reinforcement. I would rather you started with a modest goal that you can reach (remember, I said earlier that people with a high need for achievement set moderate goals so they don't frustrate themselves and can feel successful) than start off with twenty minutes a day and after a few weeks give it up.

You might ask if you get the same benefits from a three-minute session as from fifteen minutes. The answer is no, definitely not. But you will benefit from the shorter session, and when you are under unusual stress or facing a tough decision, you can spend more time in your session.

Three minutes a day will give you important results. You will create inner space for yourself. In three minutes you can do all you would do in a longer session: your "Light Touch" cue, Positive Programming, floating, visiting your haven, talking with your "wise friend," contemplative listening. Naturally, you can't do all the activities each session, whether it's long or short. But in each session, three minutes or longer, you start with your "Light Touch" cue and end with your Positive Programming message. In addition, if you're feeling out of sorts—down, upset, hurt, humiliated, fearful, pressed for time, perfectionistic—then in your session ask what statements and messages you are giving yourself to cause your feeling.

Start with your three-minute sessions today and make it a regular routine, even if things are going well in your life. Remember that many people unconsciously undermine or sabotage their success. Read your newspaper for a small sample of what I mean. I subscribe to several out-of-town newspapers, and just casting my mind back a few weeks, I can remember the following: a large developer is indicted; four county commissioners are relieved of their duties by the governor; a president of a university is asked to leave because of misappropriation of funds; a highly paid executive is forced to resign because of failure to file income taxes; two judges are declared unfit to serve because of alleged misconduct; a newspaper columnist becomes the lead story on local TV stations for allegedly soliciting a prostitute; an executive overreaches and is fired and indicted. I could go on for several pages with this dreary chronicle and still be merely skimming off the top. You see it in your newspapers and on television. The dramatic cases don't, of course, begin to represent the numbers of us who sabotage ourselves in less newsworthy ways by constant criticism of self and others, becoming easily discouraged, ignoring the "blessedness of our blessings," wasting time, playing "ain't it awful," and by being a problem to ourselves in many different and ingenious ways.

Creative Meditation will not keep you from all misadventure, but it will help you to stop and take inventory, think things through, and avoid pitfalls. It most assuredly will safeguard you from having to make the age-old lament "I don't know what I was thinking at the time," or "What could have been going through my mind?" Creative Meditation will also make it unnecessary for you to use the phrase of those who hurt themselves and others by spoiling what could have been productive and happy times. When these people come to their senses, they wonder, "How could I have been so mean over something so unimportant?"

Three minutes a day in Creative Meditation will change your life. You will create a place of peace and quiet for yourself, a place of silence where you can find reality. You will be able to hear yourself and sense the full meaning of what you say. You can examine your goals, find what you think and believe, and start treating yourself and others more kindly. If you are a type A[1] person, just for example, you can work on your feeling of always battling the clock; you can slow yourself down and become more effective. You can give yourself Positive Programming that allows you to work on one task at a time and set more realistic goals. You can decide to increase the moments you enjoy, get closer to your real self, a self that will become very important to you.

Your three-minute sessions can come at the time when you first awaken, or perhaps you can read your newspaper a little faster and use the time saved. If you work at home, take the three minutes before your second cup of coffee; if you're at the office, close the door and do it before you start work or just before you start for home. Treat it as something you are doing for yourself, a gift you give yourself. Don't tell yourself you don't have the time. If presidents can take the time for golf or a swim or to walk in the woods at Camp David, you can also take some time off. Schedule your Creative Meditation sessions the same time each day so it becomes a routine you won't forget.

Start with Your "Light Touch" Cue and End with Positive Programming

Start your three-minute Creative Meditation session the way you start your full and instant sessions by very lightly touching your thumb and forefinger together to form a circle. As you are doing this, remind yourself to take a light touch toward life and relax all over.

If you have a problem, ask what you are telling yourself about it. What statements are you making to yourself about your life, career, marriage, children,

---

1. Meyer Friedman and Ray H. Rosenman, *Type A Behavior and Your Heart* (New York: Fawcett Publishing Co.).

goals, how you should spend your time, and about other areas in your life that may be causing you trouble. Ask if you are telling yourself the *whole* truth about these areas. No matter who you are or what you're doing, these scheduled minutes of tranquillity and contemplative reflection will renew and relax you.

You must end your session with either a Positive Programming message you have selected from chapter V or a Positive Programming message you have made up for yourself. In addition, you must repeat this message many times during the day so it will become part of you. It goes without saying that the message you select is one you believe in; you remind yourself of something you believe in but tend to forget.

For example, one woman I know has as her primary Positive Programming message "Don't make it important." She repeats it to herself during the day when problems arise. She says that this Positive Programming has gradually made a significant change in her approach to life. She told me:

I used to blow everything out of proportion. Whether it was a disagreement with my husband, the children not minding or involved in an incident at school, or even missing an appointment, I would magnify it, tell myself that something bad had happened, and feel threatened. Now I have two statements I tell myself: "Don't make it important," and if I feel threatened, I tell myself, "It's only disagreeable and I can handle that." It's surprising how much those two short statements help me.

It's not surprising, really. Those two short statements contain a wealth of philosophy; but as in a shipwreck at sea, you don't explain the fine points of navigating a lifeboat but merely yell, "Man the boats;"

so you condense your philosophy into terse commands. This reminds you not to forget your philosophy.

Another woman gave herself "Permission to relax and enjoy." This woman is a vice-president of a bank. She told me, "For the first time in my life I'm able to relax and enjoy the present moment. I've given myself *permission* to work without feeling effort or tenseness. Why, I even take weekends off without feeling guilty about it or that I'm falling behind."

We Must Decide

Only you and I, of course, can decide to set aside at least three minutes a day to commune with ourselves in silence, away from the clamor of the noisy, chattering world. And in that silence only you and I, each of us alone, can become aware of ourselves, the life we lead, and the full sense and meaning of our inner talks with ourselves.

Our job, our home life, our friends and family, the world with its crimes and wars, all shriek for our attention until there is no time left for ourselves, no time to center ourselves, no time to remember the central fact on which we base our lives, no time to listen for our predominant theme. We postpone real-life living, quiet, contemplative living with a sense of direction and purpose until some time in the future, and then, often, it is too late.

We must have quiet minutes when we *listen* to ourselves, hear our spirit, our essence, and decide who we are and what we want to do. They must be minutes during which we nurture, love, and strengthen ourselves.

Start today practicing your "Light Touch" cue and

the relaxation that goes with it. Turn back to chapter V and select a Positive Programming message that best suits you. Repeat the message and think about it in your Creative Meditation session. Give yourself your message many times during the day. During your session listen to your inner messages and change those that are not worthy of your vision and your ideal; discard those that are not life- giving and life expanding. As James Allen said:

Cherish your visions; cherish your ideals;
Cherish the music that stirs in your heart,
The beauty that forms in your mind, the
Loveliness that drapes your purest thoughts,
For out of them will grow all delightful conditions,
All heavenly environment; of these, if you but
Remain true to them, your world will at last be built.

ABOUT THE AUTHOR

Dr. Nelson Boswell holds degrees from Harvard and Florida Atlantic University. As a university professor and dean he has taught graduate students, businessmen and women, and teachers working on advanced degrees. He has lectured and held seminars for various groups, including educators, businessmen and women, sales and marketing executives, and teachers. For the past eighteen years he has written a column on self-understanding for *Telephony*, the magazine of the telephone industry. For the past nineteen years he has researched, written, and narrated a nationally syndicated radio program on psychology and self-help subjects (including self-understanding, human relations, motivation, and communication) that has helped and inspired millions. Dr. Boswell lives with his wife and three children in Tampa, Florida.